ADVANCE PRAISE

Pillar-Based Marketing represents a true inflection point of technology and sophisticated marketing tactics that marketers should embrace in a digital-first world. This is the next-level blend of art and science that marketers didn't know they needed.

—NATE SKINNER, CMO AT ONFIDO

Go-to-Market strategy is so important that I wrote a book and launched a business solely focused on it. Pillar-Based Marketing has taken the organic part of GTM out of the black box and made it a critical factor to drive ongoing transformational change in every company and give marketers a seat at the C-Suite table.

—SANGRAM VAJRE, CEO OF GTM PARTNERS, BESTSELLING AUTHOR, AND PREVIOUSLY CO-FOUNDER OF TERMINUS

Dare I say keywords are dead? To be competitive in modern SEO, you've got to do right by the customer. That means going beyond keywords and considering context. I have been practicing a variation of Pillar-Based Marketing for 5+ years and firmly believe it's the most effective way to generate revenue through organic search.

—MJ PETERS, VP OF MARKETING AT COLAB SOFTWARE

I am amazed at the success we've had with Pillar-Based Marketing! Pillar-Based Marketing is key for a successful SEO and content marketing strategy. Ryan and Toph have proven that their methodology works, and they share all of their secrets in this book.

—ADAM HELWEH, CEO OF SECRET SUSHI

The complexity of understanding customer behavior gets exponentially more difficult every day. The methods in this book to efficiently align with customers and go to market will separate the winners from the losers.

—STEPHEN MESSER, CO-FOUNDER OF COLLECTIVE[I]
AND PREVIOUSLY CO-FOUNDER AND CEO OF
LINKSHARE (ACQUIRED BY RAKUTEN)

Good content marketing strategies do not aim to appeal to search engines, they appeal to real people asking real questions. Answer those questions, use common language, and make it interesting.

—NICK WOJDYLA, CMO AT BELDEN

Toph and Ryan are pioneers in an increasingly complex world of content and SEO. Pillar-Based Marketing is the evolution of decade-old generally accepted SEO principles. The modern marketing leader needs to know how their customer thinks—and make content that rises above the noise.

—IAN FAISON, CEO AT CASPIAN STUDIOS

We work with CEOs and CMOs in dozens of markets throughout the US. Every one of them is trying to figure out how to organically attract more customers efficiently. Understanding what your customers are actually thinking, and aligning to that, is the differentiator with Pillar-Based Marketing.

—MATT HUNCKLER, CEO AT POWDERKEG

PILLAR-BASED MARKETING

RYAN BROCK AND
CHRISTOPHER "TOPH" DAY

PILLAR-
BASED
MARKETING

A Data-Driven Methodology for SEO and Content That Actually Works

LIONCREST
PUBLISHING

PILLAR-BASED MARKETING
A Data-Driven Methodology for SEO and Content That Actually Works

FIRST EDITION

ISBN   978-1-5445-3981-2   *Hardcover*
        978-1-5445-3980-5   *Paperback*
        978-1-5445-3979-9   *Ebook*

CONTENTS

FOREWORD

BY HEIKE NEUMANN

I have spent many years marketing marketing software to marketers to do better marketing. Not only is this a tongue twister, but it is also a blessing and a curse. Hey, I'm a marketer, so I am my target audience, which means I know how my target audience works and thinks, and what's keeping them up at night. But being a marketer, I also know that everyone in my audience will see right through the mechanics of any lead capture, lead nurture, or lead progression program. We marketers are a very challenging target audience! We're also an audience that is notorious for being early adopters of new technology, platforms, media, content—you name it.

All of this means that, having been in B2B marketing for thirty years, I have seen strategies and tactics come and go. For over a decade now, we have been hearing that most of the buying journey is made online before a potential customer even talks to a salesperson. The percentages range from 60–80%. No matter which number is correct (if that is even measurable precisely), we see that it is happening and experience it in our own behavior.

Where we used to be focused on gathering leads, scoring them, and moving them through the sales funnel stages, now it seems that this system doesn't work any longer. So what changed?

First, people are no longer willing to freely give their contact data for every shred of information, which means you, the marketer, don't know who you are dealing with. But two other areas are making the traditional lead capture and lead progression processes fall short. First, buyers are researching in their own ways and not necessarily following the paths we marketers want to prescribe. And second, in B2B environments, buying decisions are made by buying groups. Not every person in a buying group participates in the process from beginning to end. They have "buying jobs" to finish, and they might fade in and out of the process. They might not be the decision maker, but they might be the unnamed influencer of the buying decision (maybe the one throwing a wrench in the deal that you thought you had almost closed.) You can read more about this in the third chapter of this book.

In the past, you might have come across the terms "big-net fishing" for high-level top-of-funnel demand generation activities or "small-net fishing" for very targeted demand generation activities. That translates into you, the marketer, creating a path for your audience to follow once you get them in your net through advertising, paid search, or your website. That approach would require you to know exactly who your audience is and where they will look for information so that you can target them, or "cast your net."

As we have already discovered, the whole fishing thing doesn't really work anymore. As people start looking for information in different ways, you need to create a web of information with answers to all conceivable questions that might come up regarding your value proposition, solution, or product—to help people complete their buying job. Your sales team might be talking to two or three people directly in a buying process. But in reality, six to ten people are involved in this process, and every single one is taking an individual approach to get the information they need to get their job done (hint: they are not waiting for you to present it to them).

Toph, Ryan, and I have spent hours discussing how to get into your audience's hands the information you want them to have as they finish their buying jobs.

This is where Pillar-Based Marketing enters the stage. Think of word-association games, mind maps—or spiderwebs if you want to stay with the animal analogies. I like to think about breadcrumb trails. You get your information out there so your audience can easily find it, but you also need to offer them a path to the next answer to the question they haven't even thought to ask.

Welcome to the new world, where every question has an answer…and a next question.

Heike Neumann is a data-driven B2B marketer to the core. She has extensive experience in the tech industry, working in Europe and the United States, marketing to audiences on six continents (you might guess which one isn't on the list).

INTRODUCTION

This is a book about "what ifs."

What if your website traffic increased by 10x, your leads increased by over 4x, and your customers increased by over 3x? What if you could be certain you could maintain these increases over time?

What if your cost per lead decreased by 3x—and stayed there?

What if the research you conducted as a content marketing leader found its way to the board meeting of a Fortune 100 company, and they used it to inform their ten-year strategy?

What if that Fortune 100 company acquired your startup because your content signaled you as such a powerful thought leader in their industry?

What if you could unseat the biggest names in your industry with just a few pieces of content? What if powerhouses like Microsoft, Nike, Oracle, SalesForce, HubSpot, and Amazon were showing up below your company, no matter its size, in search engine rankings for the topics that drive your business—even for topics those companies have traditionally owned?

What if you could get bonuses, promotions, and raises again and again because the actions you were taking to develop your content strategy were elevating the organization's performance across the board?

What if you were offered a seat at the table—a voice in the running of the organization at the highest level—because the work you were doing around content marketing was so powerful in driving the bottom line?

These aren't fantasies. They're not wishful thinking. They're outcomes we have seen over and over, across industries and sectors, for internal marketing leaders at organizations and owners of content marketing agencies. They are proven realities.

What if they could be realities for you?

DROWNING IN INFORMATION WITHOUT A PADDLE

Sometimes, we share these outcomes with marketers, and they listen politely, but we can tell they don't quite believe us—and that's understandable. Their experience with content marketing (especially SEO content) has been very different, full of anxiety and wasted time and effort. They are smart, capable people working overtime to make a difference to the bottom line, but they just don't have the right tools.

The modern business world is run by data. Sales, distribution, logistics, strategy: it's all data-driven. Marketing is no exception. Over the past ten years or so, the amount of data available to marketers has increased exponentially—and then increased exponentially again, and again. Marketers are neck-deep in data. Clicks, backlinks, views, impressions, search rankings. Leads. Conversions. Followers. Hashtags. Traffic. The list of possible data points a marketer might consider in determining their strategy and evaluating their success just keeps growing.

But up to now, no one has figured out which information actually matters in creating a content strategy or how to make sense of that data to make decisions. You can gather all the data you want, but if you don't have access to the right tool and methodology to make sense of it to get the results you want, it's not doing you any good. Marketers are drowning in information without a paddle.

A spreadsheet with a million data points is worthless if it can't tell you what topics to write about or how to write about them. If you can look at all this information and still not know where to start, what strategies to prioritize, or what content will engage the customers you want to attract, it's useless.

The problem is that we, as a marketing community, have come to accept uncertainty and waste as unchangeable realities of our work.

Waiting six months or a year or even more to determine whether a piece of content will reach Page One in the search rankings? That's just how it is. Writing dozens of pieces of content and hoping that at least a couple of them will generate traffic? Nothing we can do about that. Creating content across lots of different topics because we don't know which ones will engage the customers we want? Spending and spending on paid strategies because they are the only reliable generators of traffic? Crossing our fingers and hoping that at least some of the multiple campaigns we're running will result in leads? Welcome to content marketing.

We are here to show you that the pain you are experiencing no longer has to be a part of your daily routine. You don't have to wait to see whether your content performs. You don't have to throw good money after bad tactics. You don't have to guess or follow your gut about what topics to write about or how to structure your content to ensure deep engagement.

What you need is a methodology that tells you which data to use, how to make sense of it, and how to use it to determine quantifiable, defensible action steps.

Pillar-Based Marketing (PBM) is that methodology.

THE CONFIDENCE OF A PROVEN METHODOLOGY

As you read this book, you might notice that we sound very sure of ourselves. We share our experiences as facts, and we promise that if you do what we outline here, you are going to have exponentially better results than you are used to. You might hear some ideas from us that surprise or shock you, that run counter to everything you thought you knew about content marketing, especially when it comes to developing content designed to drive organic traffic from search engines.

So let us reassure you up front: we won't say a single thing that the data isn't telling us to say. We won't share one idea that hasn't worked for company after company in industry after industry. Everything we will share has been demonstrated over and over. We've spent nearly three years testing, experimenting, and reiterating this process until it works every time for every company that follows it. We arrived at these best practices through the scientific method—which means we failed, and then got better, and then got better again, until we were confident that we had found something real.

The upside of discovering something truly new is that it has the potential to offer outsized, almost unbelievable results. Even we had trouble believing what we were seeing when we first started testing this process.

The difficulty with discovering something new is that it can be difficult to let go of old ways of doing things. The pull of "doing what we've always done" can be powerful. It feels safe. So before you go forward, we encourage you to look again at that list of "what ifs." Are you getting those kinds of outcomes from your current strategies?

If not, PBM has the potential to revolutionize your work. All it requires is a mindset shift in how you think about content and the data available to you to drive it.

GETTING TO PAGE ONE

This book will teach you how to exponentially and dramatically improve the results you're getting with your organic content marketing—so much so that your content marketing strategies and insights will start to transform all your other marketing work as well.

We've gotten these outcomes for customer after customer, in every market and industry and across all types and sizes of organizations. In doing this work, we've discovered that success in content marketing is based on four foundational concepts. This book will teach you how to understand and apply these concepts to get outcomes you currently don't believe are even possible.

PAGE ONE RANKINGS

The first and most important foundational truth we will address in this book is that content *must* rank on Page One of search results in order to drive the business outcomes you care about. This concept is so critical that we're going to get dramatic with it and capitalize Page One every time we mention it. Google is actively experimenting with implementing continuous scrolling for Search Engine Results Pages, so you can trade the designation "Page One" for "Top Ten" or "above the fold" or whatever sounds accurate to you; what matters is the first ten pages that show up in search results are where the lion's share of organic traffic goes. It's the destination we're focused on, and like any city or country you visit, it's worthy of those big letters. More than 90% of all clicks occur on Page One, mostly in the first few results on Page One, so if your content is not there, it can't do its job of bringing people to your site, your solution, or your products. There are tons of other available metrics or ways of assessing the performance of your content, but they don't matter if you're not on Page One.

As we like to say, the name of the game is "Page One or bust!"

Content that gets to and stays on Page One is the only appre-

ciating asset in marketing because it continues to bring yc customers and sales without any additional money, time, or resources. We will show you not only how vital it is to be on Page One, but how to get there—and stay there—consistently and predictably, for all the topics that drive your business.

QUANTIFIABLE ORGANIC ALIGNMENT

Ranking on Page One doesn't happen because you talk about your products and how great they are. Content ranks on Page One because it addresses the needs, problems, pains, desires, and questions of the real individuals who search the internet— and the real journeys they take in learning about and buying products and services. Exponential growth in outcomes for your content marketing requires you to be organically aligned with those needs, questions, and journeys.

Organic alignment means that you flip your approach: you start with a complete understanding of what customers actually want and are already talking about, and how they are talking about it, and then you write content that matches what you learn. **We will show you exactly how to organically align with customers, how to quantifiably prove that you have done so, and how to leverage that alignment into content that goes to Page One quickly.**

BEHAVIORAL NETWORKS

Organic alignment to customer behavior can only happen when you have a complete picture of the real-world search behavior of the customers you want to reach. Previous tools and approaches have attempted to align with customers based on internally generated lists of keywords and terms. Not only does this keep the focus on your needs (instead of customers' needs), but it also fails to reflect the complex, interconnected, nonlinear web of behaviors that real people engage in when they search for solutions to their problems or answers to their questions.

Instead of hoping customers come to you, you need to be where they already are, and that requires insight into the entire complex network of search behaviors, including the "hubs" or connection points among different search journeys. Another word for these connection points is "pillars," which is why that word is front and center in the title of this book and the methodology it teaches. **We will introduce you to the complexity of customers' real-world buying journeys and show you how to select the pillars you are interested in and write content that will engage readers exactly where they need you.**

ACTIONABLE DATA

As we mentioned above, marketers have access to an amount of data that has never before existed in the history of the world—but unless you can use that data to get on Page One and drive the business results you want, it's not just not useful. It's actually a problem. The more data you have that doesn't help you, the faster you drown: there are too many options, too many possible approaches, too many topics you could write about, and too many ways you could write about each one. Suddenly, a task as apparently simple as choosing a title for a blog post can become a battle of "my instincts versus yours" or a scramble to cover every possible topic that customers might ever search.

Actionable data, on the other hand, is information that tells you *what to prioritize, where to start, and how to proceed*. The

PBM approach, based on the complete network of real-world search behavior, pinpoints you to the exact strategies to use—down to the specific topics, titles, words, and headings to put in your blog posts. **We will give you step-by-step instructions for identifying what to write about, how to write about it, and how to publish it to get immediate customer engagement that drives bottom-line results.**

THE BLOG POST THAT CHANGED EVERYTHING

For a lot of marketers, this approach represents a complete shift in mindset from what they are currently doing.

We understand—the same thing happened to us.

Just a few years ago, Ryan was running a content marketing agency and barely sleeping at night because of the anxiety of never being able to know ahead of time what content would succeed, or whether customers would stick with him long enough to find out. Toph was a serial entrepreneur with decades of experience running one company after another who was wondering whether marketing could ever be anything but a complete waste of money.

We'd used all of the traditional approaches. We'd seen fads come and go. We were struggling in the land of waste and anxiety, just like so many marketers still do today. Without realizing it, we were both independently seeking the solution to these problems: Ryan at his marketing agency and Toph in his data-driven marketing business.

And then…

One day, at a meeting, one of Toph's data analysts asked a question. He looked at the complex search data the company was using to help customers drive better marketing outcomes, and he asked, "Could we apply this to content?" And Toph said, "That's a great idea. Let's try it."

The team got together, gathered data, and wrote a single blog post. One post. And that post got to Page One in four days and stayed there. For years. Without an edit. Without a paid bump. It just stayed and stayed and stayed, driving traffic and customers because it was *completely and perfectly aligned* with what customers were actually searching for, and wanting to learn, about the topic.

That's when Toph knew he was onto something. But he also knew he needed a partner, an expert in the content writing itself, someone who could take the incredible, network-based data they were working with and turn it into world-class content.

Enter Ryan.

When Ryan and his team saw the network data and what it could tell them about how to write content, they literally couldn't believe it was true. They couldn't believe the results they were seeing. But then it happened again. And again. It happened often enough, and was predictable enough, that we brought our companies together to do this work. Over several years, we tested the approach, developed the best practices, refined the data analysis, and built the platform to manage and drive it all.

And now we get to share it with you.

Throughout this book, you'll learn a lot more about our origin story, how we developed this approach and the data that drives it, and how to apply our best practices to your own content. We just want you to know: we were exactly where you are now, and we built this process and the technology behind it from the ground up to address exactly the problems you are having now, and we have seen it work for companies from startups to Fortune 100 companies in B2B, B2C, PLG, and in every industry.

In every single case, adopting this methodology has utterly transformed the results these customers were getting—and we are thrilled to be starting the same journey with you.

GETTING THERE

In this book, we will lead you through everything you need to understand, apply, and reap the benefits of the Pillar-Based Marketing approach.

Section 1 will take you through our backstories and how we ended up working together, including the frustrations and problems we were dealing with that became the motivation for Pillar-Based Marketing. We will show you exactly what isn't working with current content marketing approaches, how to shift your mindset, what PBM is, and how it addresses every anxiety you have about the performance of your content.

Section 2 offers the "how-to" of PBM. It offers clear action steps for implementing PBM in your own work, shows how the PBM methodology will radically improve your outcomes, and demonstrates how to turn search data into quantifiably effective content that ranks on Page One in days or weeks, not months or years.

Short version: there is a way to get results you can only dream of—and continue driving those results with a methodology that is every bit as clear as the principles you apply to other digital marketing tactics like paid digital, email marketing, and even Account-Based Marketing. We are getting those results right now, for our own business and for customer after customer who uses our methodology.

But not so long ago, that wasn't the case at all.

SECTION ONE

WHY PILLAR-BASED MARKETING?

CHAPTER 1

MARKETERS DON'T SLEEP

Hello! It's Ryan. Later in the book, Toph and I are going to tell you exactly what we've discovered about content marketing and SEO and how you can apply it to revolutionize what you're doing. That's not blowing smoke; we're going to deliver on a provable, actionable data-driven promise.

But before we get to that, we wanted to give you a backstage look at how and why we got where we are today. Because this wasn't a miracle. Our success didn't come out of nowhere. It was the result of painful, sleepless nights and years of knowing that somewhere, somehow, there had to be a better way—and then working tirelessly to figure out what that better way might be.

We started with our organic content strategies exactly where you are right now: drowning in spreadsheets, exhausted, uncertain, and anxious because we just didn't know whether what we were doing was working.

This chapter tells my story. It takes place in 2016 when I was running my own content marketing agency, working with Fortune 100 clients, leading a team of highly skilled and capable writers, delivering world-class work in line with the campaigns our customers were undertaking. Like marketers across all kinds of other industries and organizations, we were doing exceptionally well by every available metric.

And yet.

Every night I lay awake running numbers. Every night I wondered if the company could last another six months, if I could make payroll, if customers would fire us—and it had nothing to do with the quality of our work. For a long time, I thought I was alone, but when I talked to friends and colleagues in marketing, whether they ran their own agencies or worked internally at companies large or small, they were all feeling the same way. It turns out that the problem wasn't us. The problem was content marketing itself.

TOPH SAYS

Hey, everyone, just a little note here.

This is a great story that Ryan is telling. But since it's from his perspective as a person running his own marketing agency, it might seem like it doesn't apply to you if you're an internal marketer at a company.

Not true.

We've worked with thousands of CEOs and marketers in dozens of industries, and every stakeholder we've talked to has struggled with these same issues.

Marketers may not always want to talk about them with their CEO, but that's another story. When marketers get together, whether they're in an agency or inside a company, these are the stories they tell.

WILL THEY STICK WITH US?

Like I did most evenings, on this particular evening, I was sitting on the couch with my wife, watching a movie. We didn't have our son then, so it was just the two of us, and I was trying to enjoy our time together. But I wasn't really there. I had a drink in one hand and my phone in the other, open to the calculator, and while I kept one eye on the movie, I was actually crunching the numbers.

My team had spent the last week preparing for a meeting with a huge client. We'd already had a number of back-and-forth debates with them about strategy, and tomorrow's meeting was the decision point. We would have to finally decide on how to move the campaign forward.

As a result, neither the plight of the movie's hero nor even the looks my wife was giving me could distract me from running a series of worst-case scenarios. I couldn't help thinking about what would happen if we went into the meeting and heard that terrible phrase: "It's just not going to work." What if our contact, or the marketing committee, or the VP just didn't agree with what we were proposing? I'd only signed this client a few months before—a major pharmaceutical company that represented a huge step up for my agency—and already I was considering how I'd make payroll if they fired us.

The reality is, even though they were a big client, I went through the same exercise with every customer. Without even pulling up the spreadsheets, I could see all the numbers, every single customer we had, how much they paid, how long they had left on their contracts. And I went through every scenario. If we lost this or that customer, how would that impact mid-month payrolls? What would it look like in 45 days? I would add up the numbers and see that in the worst case, it might not be enough. So I'd look at all the sales and deals I had in the pipeline, or at least my mind's best image of those things. What was a sure thing, and what might fall through? Which customers would be patient and understand that this work takes time, commitment, and a willingness to wait and see results? Which customers were new or didn't yet believe in our approach?

I ran the numbers over and over in my head, punching scenarios into the calculator, thinking through every "what if." Eventually, I arrived at a point where I wasn't happy exactly, but I felt like we would probably be okay for now.

At that moment I suddenly realized it had gone very quiet. The movie was over. My wife had gone to bed. The TV was off, the room was dark, and I hadn't even noticed any of that happening.

I dragged myself to bed as well, took my anxiety and sleeping medications, and slowly managed to fall asleep…only to wake up again at 3:00 a.m., heart pounding, grabbing for the phone, running through it all one more time.

Now, I know that some of these are issues that all business owners deal with, but I had a much bigger problem: my agency did content marketing, and content marketing is a business tailor-made to cause anxiety.

It's not that we didn't know what we were doing—as I mentioned, our client roster had many Fortune 100 clients. I employed world-class writers and a unique approach to content development that was working (at least) as well as any other existing content strategy.

The problem was the uncertainty.

Even with the best team and strategy in the world, it was simply not possible to predict whether a specific content marketing campaign would be successful, or how soon. That was, and is, the deep anxiety at the heart of content marketing.

For the companies that believed in us, that stuck around long enough to see results, we were delivering exceptional value. But unlike every other area of modern business, content marketing had no reliable data, no way to design a strategy with any certainty that it would drive results. We had to rely on what we, the client and my team, collectively thought was a good starting point for content topics and SEO keywords to target. Every campaign was an exercise in waiting and hoping, sometimes as long as six months or a year, to see if our hunch was right, or if we could gain a clear direction about what elements of our hunch were wrong. A lot of clients just weren't willing to commit to that. In the modern business world, six months is an eternity. And taking six months to possibly, or actually probably, find out that only 10% of what we'd published amounted to anything? Forget about it.

So there I was, up at 3:00 a.m., running scenarios. I knew my alarm would go off in three hours, that I wouldn't be at full power, and that yet again I had wasted my whole evening on this. But I couldn't help it. With no way to prove to clients that what we were doing would work, I was always living on borrowed time. I was stuck wondering to myself, "Will they stick with us long enough to see results?"

And that's to say nothing of what my wife had to endure as her husband sat there, present only physically, night in and night out.

YOUR INSTINCTS OR MINE?

After dozing for what felt like minutes, I woke up groggy and jittery at 6:00, and by 7:00, I was already at the office. I had an hour or two to wander and fret, and then at about 10:00, we all piled into our cars and headed to the client's office.

We rode mostly in silence. Everyone was nervous about the meeting. This was not only a big and important client but a client we had a lot of respect for. Our main contact, Allison, was a woman living with the disease the company was trying to help patients manage, and she was smart and capable and a real advocate for herself and other patients. I liked her a lot.

We'd been going through this back-and-forth process for so long, though, that everyone was frustrated. It was maybe even more frustrating because there really wasn't anyone to blame. She was doing what she thought was best, and we were doing what we thought was best, and nobody in this mix had complete confidence that we were doing the right thing.

The frustration was even worse because the beginning of the relationship had been smooth and easy. We'd started by developing the so-called "down-funnel" pieces of content, the landing pages, e-books, and other tools potential customers could access to learn more about the product and put it to better use once they'd engaged with the company. That kind of content was easy to create because it was based on the company's domain knowledge and was designed for customers or potential customers who were already engaged with the company and wanted to learn more.

Where we struggled was in creating the blogs that were supposed to bring customers in initially: the organic content. Organic content goes out into the world of the internet and draws people in, typically from search engines. It is supposed to meet people throughout their journey, when they're trying to find solutions, find answers, and understand how to live their lives better. Its job is to pull potential customers toward the company's solution. And that's where we, like all marketers, were having a problem, because no one could really know which pieces of organic content would work until you put them out there on the internet and waited to see if customers actually saw them and how they would respond.

In other words, when it came to developing and writing that organic content, it was totally a question of instincts. What do you instinctively believe will work? What do you feel your customers will respond to? And often, the best apparent place to start is with that domain expertise that drove the down-funnel content; if we think people will value those pieces of content, the topics they enter during their search will be the same ones. Right?

The challenge here, as with all new content marketing initiatives, was that our contact's instincts about the blog content were at odds with what we were finding in our rudimentary keyword research. More than that, her instincts were subject to the instincts of the marketing committee she reported to. Too many cooks and all that.

Going into the meeting with our contact, I had to decide: do I try to talk her out of following her instincts so she can follow mine? Or maybe it would be better if I deferred to the client's best guess and said, "You tell us what to do, and we'll do it."

There were no tools or data to definitively answer these questions, so despite all our good intentions and our mutual respect as professionals, we were going into this meeting adversarial. She wanted to know why we were taking so long to implement the plan her company had provided, whereas I was trying to convince her that the company should let us go in an entirely different direction.

I was ready for a "come to Jesus" moment. I wanted us to finally make a decision one way or the other, to choose her instincts or mine.

I told her that my team had spent hours poring over the customer interviews and other materials she'd sent us. We'd gone through the plan. We'd done our research. And based on what was available to us, we didn't believe we should make the changes the company was asking for.

I was upfront with her about the realities. I told her that I couldn't promise her that everything we were doing was right, only that our instinct was close enough, or at least more broadly informed. That something we were doing was right, and the direction she and the company were asking for was not.

Most importantly, I asked her to let us get the content out there so we could start collecting data. Then we could see which pieces were getting engagement, which pieces people were clicking on, and which were driving real leads. If we could get some content out in the world, then it would become less about our instincts. At that point, we could shift toward doing what the data told us the customers liked, so we could do more of that in the future.

So there it was: her instincts or mine? Should we use the company's preplanned campaign or trust my team's content and put it out into the world to succeed or fail?

It was an incredibly tense moment. There would be absolutely no way to know whether we'd made the right choice for at least several months, maybe closer to a year, when we could finally see how customers actually responded to the content. Not one single effective tool existed to tell us ahead of time how to make the decision one way or the other. And with the budget for this initiative only barely approved in the first place, asking to spend some of that budget on what could be perceived as wasted, dead-end content was a tough ask.

The team sat in silence, waiting for the fate of our efforts to be decided.

Finally, Allison looked at me and said, "You know what? I think you're right. This is what we need to do."

We had won! This was the biggest victory we could have hoped for, especially with a new customer, that they trusted us enough to choose my instincts over their own. Elated and relieved, the team packed up our computers and backpacks and got ready to head back to the office. We were excited to finally get started on the campaign.

I was celebrating with them, but I could also feel the anxiety building again in the pit of my stomach. Now we were completely responsible for the success or failure of this campaign, and we'd have no way to know whether my instincts were right for at least six months.

And just as we were leaving, Allison said, "Oh, by the way, I'll just need to run this by the committee. I'll email you guys later in the day to let you know."

DEATH BY COMMITTEE

By the time we got back to the office, our victory was already over. The committee, which wasn't involved in any of the research, didn't attend the meeting, and weren't part of our conversations, operating totally in a vacuum, decided that what we were doing was counter to their domain expertise—their instincts—and what they thought had worked in the past. So they forced Allison to come back to us and say no to all of our ideas. We were to go ahead with their original redirect to our planned campaign, make the changes and edits they wanted, and put that content out.

All I could think was what a lot of wasted effort there'd been on all sides. I couldn't even blame them. Everybody has their own experiences, background, and expertise to believe their position is correct. Especially when it comes to something as nebulous as determining what your target market of ideal customers will actually be interested in and searching for online. No one really knew at the time what would work, so one person's guess was as good as another's—or as bad.

What really bothered me was the effect on my team. They were being pulled in so many different directions with no tools to help them get closer to knowing what their readers actually cared about. They had no way to validate or defend their work. They had to write and rewrite campaigns based on what seemed like whims, their own or someone else's. As a result, a lot of their time, effort, and work was just wasted, not to mention the time and effort on the client side. And this was just one client. We had dozens of other clients, and it was the same dynamic with most of them, pushing and pulling and never being clear about where we were headed.

The good news was that we didn't lose the client that day. We created the content they wanted and got it out there. All that hand-wringing, all my anxiety the night before, all the back and forth, was just wasted time.

The bad news was that we did lose the client a few months later. There wasn't even time to see whether the campaign would have worked. They went in a different direction before the data could even come in, a pretty typical outcome in a corporate world where six months is just too long to wait for results. So in the end, this really was death by committee, although we didn't quite know it at the time.

The weird thing about uncertainty, though, is that it works both ways. That was brought home to me in a perfectly ironic twist almost at the very moment we heard from Allison that the committee had nixed our idea.

A TOSS OF THE COIN

Back to that fateful day and the decision to just do what the client wanted. I'd broken the news to the team, gotten them as calmed down as possible, and set them to work on the approved campaign. At least we had a clear direction, and I could feel the energy in the office settle and engage as the writers adjusted to the change and got down to it.

Just as I sat back down at my desk, the phone rang.

On the other end was one of our major B2B clients. We were developing a huge campaign for them around 401(k) products, informing employers about how a 401(k) works, why they should offer them, how to provide them to employees, that kind of thing. We'd been working on some of the long-form materials for close to six months, and they had paid us a lot of money. Now our contact (one of my all-time favorite clients, I should mention) was calling to tell me that a change in direction had come from above her in the organization, that they had shifted the terminology they wanted to use in the articles. They wanted to start using totally different language to talk about their products.

Unfortunately, they felt that they'd already invested too much in the existing pieces, so they weren't going to revise them. They were going to trash everything we'd done.

She was very apologetic, and I explained to her that I was used to this, that we saw this a lot. I told her that she was not alone. I was preparing myself for more bad news when she apologized again and dropped a totally different surprise. The decision had been made to write new materials to cover the same topics, but from scratch with the new language. She wanted to know when I could send her a quote for the new work.

She wanted me to send a work order for a whole set of new pieces that were going to be just as big as the ones we'd already written, but with slightly different language.

Part of me was frustrated because this represented another enormous waste of time for my team. Yet again, there was something completely out of our control, a whim on the client's part not driven by data or information at all, creating a total shift in direction. This time, though, the result was that I was going to get a nice, big contract out of it.

That's how the whole thing kept going: a customer's whim could lose us a contract or create months' worth of new work. It was a toss of the coin. Even as I was writing the new contract, I couldn't help thinking that there had to be a better way to do this work, some way to get the actual data to make informed choices, to reduce the terrible amount of waste and anxiety.

By the end of the day, I was wrung out. I needed to talk to someone who would understand.

IT'S NOT WORKING

My favorite dive bar was just a few blocks away, and that's where a group of us held an impromptu marketing moan session every couple of weeks. After all, who better to understand the pain of the content marketing universe than other marketers? Texting my wife that I'd be home in a couple of hours, I stepped through the door into the dim lighting of the bar, where a couple of old-fashioned TVs played sports channels, and cigarette burns still mark the tables from the time before smoking bans had cleared the air in our city. Pitchers of flat domestic light beer sat sweating on top of paper placemats designed to improve your golf game. People talked loudly in between bites of the famous wings. It was familiar and reassuring. At the corner table, three of my marketing buddies were waving to me, and I walked over and sank into my chair with a sigh.

I was so tired that instead of joining in right away, I just ordered a beer and listened to the conversation. They were in the middle of discussing a statistic one of them had heard from a coworker. Apparently, only 19% of companies believe content marketing is actually working for their business.

Let me repeat that, because it's astounding.

Fewer than 20% of companies believe that content marketing works.

Is it any surprise we're not sleeping? Can you imagine hearing that only 19% of CEOs, or sales VPs, or production managers believe that what they're doing is working?

So what is it about content marketing specifically that drives this uncertainty, this anxiety, this lack of sleep?

The problem was right there in the open. It was there in every interaction I'd had that day, and every day I ran my agency at that time. It was understood by content marketers everywhere. No one could say ahead of time what potential customers would respond to, and not even the most widely adopted SEO tools available could do much to tell you where you needed to go with your content—only what to do if you already knew your destination.

We were all out there in the wilds of the internet, fishing with content to see what we caught. Only then could we begin to gather data and make real decisions. The wasted six months or a year? That was just part of the deal. Every one of my friends at that bar, and every marketer I knew, and every so-called marketing guru in the world for that matter, we were all living with the same reality and telling these same stories of frustration, waste, and miscommunication.

After an hour or so, I drained my beer and got up to leave. The session was still going strong, but I wanted to get home so that I could hopefully get a little more sleep and be ready to do it all again the next day.

THERE HAD TO BE A BETTER WAY

As I walked back through the crowded parking lot to my car, I had a thought I'd had over and over again, more and more often recently: there had to be a better way.

I used to position my firm as the "creative writers," opposing the endless data present elsewhere in marketing. We were successful because we knew our craft, dammit, and could create a perfect tone for the perfect audience. We could make people really feel things, even about corporate marketing content. But even I had to admit that the more I'd worked with data, the better I'd gotten at writing content, feeling my way forward, and analyzing the information we did have. In turn, I had come to believe with increasing certainty that there was something there, a better way just out of my reach, an approach based on real information, a way to actually predict what content customers would read, that would drive real sales, that would rank on search engines right away and just make sense.

Every single other area of modern business had this level of knowledge. Ninety percent of the data ever generated in the history of the world had been generated in the previous two years. Google claimed to have over 100 million gigabytes of search data. The data existed. So why did it feel like content marketing was the only element of modern marketing that just didn't benefit from it?

My experience told me that I could change the very nature of my work if I could only figure out how to align with target-customer needs faster. A way to trump domain expertise and instinct and cut right to the part where we *knew* what our target customers wanted. How could we not have enough information? What was the missing piece?

Little did I know that right at that moment, in the very same city, just down the street from me, someone else was working on this exact problem—someone with the data and the experience to lead us to that better way.

CHAPTER 2

MARKETING IS A COMPLETE WASTE OF MONEY

Hey there! It's Toph. You met Ryan in the last chapter, and he'll be coming back later in the book, but for now, I'd like to share my story about how I got here. Ryan comes at the issue we are talking about in the book from the marketing side. He's also a creative expert, a storyteller. I come at this issue from the business side. I like to say what I mean, and I'm pretty much always looking at the bottom line. While Ryan was figuring out the best way to write content for customers, I was building and selling a series of businesses in just about every industry as a CEO, investment banker, and investor. As it turns out, we were both successful—but we both experienced the same exact problem.

Even as we were writing this book, I became the CEO of Elevate Ventures, the number one most active venture capital (VC) firm in the Great Lakes region and the 20th most active in the United States, according to PitchBook's Global League Tables. As the head of a VC firm, I am on the ground floor with companies across dozens of industries, and I see the same issues we are talking about in this book in virtually every company I work with, whether it's a startup, scaleup, or late-stage venture.

Ryan and I got along great right from the first moment we met, but unfortunately, that's not the reality for most marketers and CEOs, at least not if history has anything to teach us. Chief marketing officers (CMOs) have the shortest tenure of any position in the C-suite. And they often spend their whole two or three years as CMO scared of the CEO because the CEO always wants to know: *What's the bottom line?* How are you driving sales? What is marketing doing to drive qualified leads? Is your marketing bringing in actual customers? The best CMOs can answer these questions in some areas, but even as organic content has become an increasingly vital part of the modern marketing mix, it has remained hazy for all the reasons Ryan mentioned in the last chapter.

As a result, CEOs...well, I hate to say this, but they get the idea that marketing is a waste of money.

CEOs and CFOs believe that if you can't explain why they're spending money, if you can't tell them what the bottom-line results your marketing is getting, then they're not going to fund it.

That's why it's funny that I got into the marketing business at all, as the co-founder and CEO of DemandJump. Because I've run a lot of businesses, in a lot of different industries, and for most of that time, I honestly could not tell you whether any of our marketing was working. And neither could anyone else.

4,000 PINK FLIERS

I started my first business in the spring of 1989, when I was a freshman in college. It was a painting business with 14 employees, painting homes in the Chicago suburbs. We were young and had a lot of energy, and we were ready to make money, ready to paint homes for anyone who would hire us.

Of course, no one had ever heard of us. So our first step was to figure out how we would market our new business so that people would become aware of our company and hopefully select us to paint their homes.

In 1989, email may have existed somewhere, but we certainly didn't have it yet. So our marketing methodology, if you can call it that, was to go print out 4,000 fliers. That's it. We printed them on bright pink pieces of paper so they would stand out. Then we would rent a car—the cheapest car we could find with a four-cylinder engine, so we could floor it from one mailbox to the next—and we would run around, and I would hang out the window and chuck flyers into the flags of mailboxes at each of these 4,000 homes and hope that someone would call us.

The most sophisticated part of all this was that we'd target homes that looked like they could use a paint job. That was the closest thing we had to a marketing strategy.

Each time we did a campaign like this, it would take us several weekends to get all of the fliers out to these homes, and by the time we'd return the car, the brakes were burned all to hell and the car smelled like melting rubber. We'd literally burn the brake pads off going mailbox to mailbox. Even worse, my ribs were bruised from hanging out the window three weekends straight.

From those 4,000 pink fliers, we would get maybe three jobs.

Every other job we ever got was from word of mouth. Somebody experienced our service, thought that we did a good job, and at the neighborhood cocktail party, they would tell their friends that "the nicest young men" just painted their home. That's how we got all of our business.

At least, I assume that's what happened. We ended up getting a lot of jobs, but we never really knew where they came from. For three years we went out riding around, passing out thousands of pink fliers, and probably getting three or four jobs a year from them. Or maybe we got ten. I don't know.

What I do know is that we spent a lot of time, got sore ribs, and put a lot of miles on somebody else's cars with very little result. Probably those fliers helped nudge someone who later heard a good thing about us, and maybe that made them call us. But most people probably took one look and then threw the fliers in the trash. We passed out all those fliers because at the time, that's what people did, so that's what we did. And we kept doing it even though we had no idea whether the fliers were getting us business or not. We were basically throwing paper into the wind.

To be honest, I didn't really think much about it. As long as the business was growing, we had to assume that what we were doing from a marketing perspective was making a difference.

And then along came this thing called the internet.

BUILD IT AND THEY WILL COME

By 1997, I had moved on from painting houses and started a broadband company—cable, internet, and telephony. Our customers were in the multifamily sector (apartment communities, in other words), and they were tired of cable operators stringing cables across their buildings and sidewalks or not showing up on time. Our company provided better customer service, we could turn the cable on and off remotely, and we figured out how to deliver symmetrical internet speeds of 1.5 Mbps, so we really did have a better product to offer these apartment communities. I know 1.5 Mbps doesn't sound like a lot, but back then, that was lightning fast.

In terms of marketing, though, we were in exactly the same place we'd been with the painting company. How could we get the word out to people so they'd become aware of our company and what we had to offer?

The internet seemed to offer a shiny, new way of getting customers to come to us.

Websites were a new innovation, and the belief in the business world was: build it and they will come. We thought that we could just build a website that told people what we did and how great we were, and people would magically find us. Sure, there were some really early forms of SEO—we're literally talking here about someone adding a white block with white text on it to the bottom of the web page and cramming a bunch of keywords into it. But that's it. It was very rudimentary, which matched the rudimentary nature of search at the time.

We thought that was all there was to it: create a web presence, and business would roll in.

Throughout my career as a CEO, across all these businesses and industries, that's what I saw over and over again. Every time a new strategy came out in marketing, everybody started using it. So that's what we did, too. And just like we never knew how many jobs we got from those pink fliers at our painting company, we continued to not know how many real sales, or qualified leads, we were getting from our marketing efforts, no matter how supposedly sophisticated they got.

Honestly, I can't remember exactly what we had on that first website, but it doesn't matter because I have no idea now, and I had no idea then, how many people came to the site, or actually bought something because of the site, or whether the people who were coming to the site were the right people in the first place.

In the end, we sold that business to a Fortune 100 company and still had no idea what worked or didn't work in marketing.

EVERYBODY'S DOING IT

After a few years of that, people on the internet started getting savvier, and companies started to realize they had to do more than just put up a website to get customers to come to them. But still, no one knew what would actually work, so the solutions started proliferating. This was when I was running a business doing automated meter reading and utility billing software. As I mentioned earlier, I've spent time in many different sectors.

We were still working in the multifamily space, apartment communities, but now we had hardware that would individually read each apartment's utility meter and help the managers more fairly divvy up the utility billing for the entire community. And we even started selling to municipalities and investor-owned utilities.

At this point, I'd been in the painting business, the broadband business, the automated meter reading business, and the billing software business with business models that included both B2C and B2B. We'd sold to individuals, large enterprises, small enterprises, mom-and-pops, governmental entities, institutional companies—the list goes on. In every scenario, I still had the same problem I started with: how do I let people know about my company and services so they will call me and buy what I'm selling?

This was around 2003, and the solution then in vogue was supposed to be branding. This was the new silver bullet that would break through the anonymity of the internet and pull people to us: spending a bunch of money engaging an expert to design a fancy logo, develop our color palette, and curate the on-brand words that we wanted to use.

So that's what we did.

At the billing software company, we spent a $100,000 on a spiffy brand and a slick new site, and I still don't know if even one real, qualified lead came from that. Definitely a waste of money for an early-stage company, but that's what we did. We didn't want to fall behind.

We could have spent the same amount of money on any number of experiments to bring customers in. A website, branding, and keyword research seemed as likely to succeed as printing a bunch of collateral and handing it out at trade shows. Why did we choose to do one of these things over another? Because everybody did, and nobody knew any better.

When none of these options panned out as promised, more and more "silver bullets" kept appearing, with each promising to be better than the last. The next bandwagon I jumped on was hiring an agency to help us solve SEO and drive more traffic to our site. That was supposed to get customers to come to us. But we didn't really notice any material difference in qualified traffic from that, so we shifted again and compensated by focusing on paid ads around topics we cared about.

Yet again, we saw zero change. I started saying to everyone who would listen that SEO is a four-letter word because it always felt like we had to do it, and everybody was always talking about it, but it never seemed to live up to any of its promises. Agencies could charge a pretty penny on big promises, but from the start, it seemed to me that nobody could back those guarantees up with a surefire way to drive traffic and, with it, new customers.

RYAN SAYS

Ouch, Toph. This one hits pretty close to home. But, as they say, the truth hurts, and this is *definitely* the truth—especially earlier on in SEO's history. (Does anybody else still have nightmares when they hear the word "Panda"?)

Every time a new silver bullet left us wanting, we went back to the numbers game that made sense on paper, which is outbound calling. The tried-and-true "brute-force" method, it involved calling as many potential customers as possible—because we knew that some of those calls at least resulted in customers. It was high touch, but no matter what new methods we were sold on, customers simply weren't coming to us on their own. Better to come knocking ourselves than stand by and wait for nothing.

For a long time, I thought I was alone. I thought, *is this just me? Am I just bad at this marketing stuff?* Then I started an investment banking firm, and suddenly I had access to hundreds of CEOs across all kinds of industries and business models, and I realized: this isn't just me, and it's not just common. It's universal.

THE DARK OF NIGHT

It was around 2009 that I started an investment banking firm. We would talk to all sorts of companies to see if we could help them raise capital, or if they were interested in selling. I met with hundreds of CEOs from all over the country, from startups to $100 million-dollar companies. These companies were in all different industries, from SaaS to advanced manufacturing to healthcare and logistics, insurance, finance, and education.

Not one of those CEOs quantifiably knew whether or how marketing was supporting their bottom line. When we talked about go-to-market strategy, not one of them ever pointed to marketing as a driver. No CEO I met with—whether they were ready to sell or wanted help with raising capital—ever led with marketing because they didn't know how it was driving results or impacting the business.

They knew they had to do marketing. They hoped that their marketing team did some "stuff" that would work, but they never prioritized spending on marketing because they just didn't know what results it created. They didn't even know what "stuff" marketing was doing. Just like me, all they knew was that they were supposed to have marketing, so they did.

By the way, I don't think any of this is the marketers' fault.

Every other department in a company can see, hear, or touch whatever they're doing. The finance department can input a bunch of data into a piece of software and present those numbers to the CEO. In warehousing, I can see whether a box is sitting on a shelf or if it's been shipped. Even in sales, I know if I've called you and if you've returned my call.

Every department has finite data that they're putting into a piece of software to help them make better decisions, except, it would seem, for marketing. Especially any kind of marketing involving digital content.

In the old days, when I started, the problem was that I didn't know if somebody actually saw my billboard. I didn't know if they threw my flier in the trash can. I didn't know if they kept that pen with my logo on it or gave it to their kids who don't give a you-know-what about my company.

The problem now is that while marketers are smart people who care about their craft, there just hasn't been the database structure, the computational power, or the application of math with new methodologies to understand what is really happening when people are searching on the internet and engaging with content. And that puts the marketer at an unfair disadvantage.

As a result, very little has changed. In my decades of experience as a CEO, marketing has gone from literally throwing pieces of paper out of a moving car to a multibillion-dollar industry encompassing branding, trade shows, paid ads, website design, and of course, content writing, and we're still basically throwing stuff out the window and hoping somebody picks it up.

In fact, I recently found the first-ever artist's rendition of what digital marketing actually looks like online!

What happens to 90.63% of the content being written right now, across every business and industry.

To extend even more grace to my marketer colleagues, it's critical to stress that the pressure to show return on investment and pursue the lowest-cost, highest-return marketing tactics contributed to this culture. As the internet began to mature and certain digital marketing tactics showed promising signs of true measurability, smart marketers were *always* incentivized to focus their efforts accordingly. It didn't matter if something like paid search was the *best* marketing tactic for a business; what mattered was that it was knowable. For many CEOs, that measurability—the ability to know for the first time how many people saw your ads and engaged with them—felt like a huge step up. Paid advertising online was the new silver bullet.

Until it wasn't.

THE MONEY PIT

From search ads and Facebook ads to ads you place on websites you think your customers might visit, at first blush, paid ads seem like a great way to get immediate results. You pay Google, and they put your website into a nice little "Ad" box right up at the top of a search page. Straight to the top ranking. Or you place a short video on Facebook, and if somebody stops scrolling long enough to look at it, they might click through to your longer-form content. If you want to show a quick upturn in traffic to your page or clicks on your search result, paid ads are the way to go. Unlike the billboards of the past or even the burgeoning corporate blogs of recent history, at least paid strategies are measurable; you pay for a certain number of ads and get a corresponding increase in clicks and traffic.

So what could be wrong with it?

The problem, as I came to learn firsthand, is that paid strategies are a money pit.

With paid ads, you never get to *stop* paying. You rank at the top as long as you keep paying Google, or you get clicks and traffic as long as you keep paying Facebook, but the second you stop, there go your great results. This formula can work really well for certain kinds of businesses where the path from ad to purchase is short and simple. For many e-commerce brands, the go-to-market strategy can be summed up as a simple formula: if you work at it long enough, you'll figure out how much to spend on which channels to drive enough sales to make the whole endeavor profitable.

That value proposition gets harder to realize when your sales cycle becomes more complicated than selling an item in a cart on a website, though. For business-to-business (B2B) brands especially, and even business-to-consumer (B2C) brands that are selling higher-ticket items after a longer and more considered purchase experience, the transactional nature of paid advertising comes with a lot of risk.

If you spend all of your money on top-of-the-funnel search ads, for example, you end up with very little ability to guide the purchase experience further. You don't control it. You can't scale it. Whatever platform you pay to host the content decides who sees it, using algorithms they don't share. Even worse, if the search engine or social media site you're using chooses to change their policies and procedures overnight—like suddenly making it a lot harder for customers to click away from their site onto yours—there's nothing you can do about it. All the while, you have to hope your website is built just right so that, whatever ad a person clicks to find their way to you, they can find all the information they need in one place to make a purchase.

But that's just not how people buy, especially not after decades of living with smartphones in our pockets. A paid ad can be a great way to break the ice, but as people do their independent research and look for the answers they need to finally make a purchase, they can stray far from you and your website. The longer it takes for someone to find answers, the greater the chances that they won't ever find their way back to you—especially if too much of your marketing mix is focused on transactional paid advertising.

Because, again: you stop paying and it goes away, and so do the clicks and the traffic. From my perspective, trying to make the best use of a company's resources, that sounds like a bad deal. If I'm going to invest my company's money and my staff's time and energy into producing marketing materials, I feel like I should own that content and control it. I should have the ability to see each customer's journey from becoming aware of my brand to making a purchase, and I should be right there beside them at each touchpoint along the way. For the kinds of businesses I've owned and operated, achieving that kind of reach with paid ads is just too expensive.

The reason for this is simple, by the way: increased competition and a limited selection of platforms.

Going into 2022, research firm IAB (the Interactive Advertising Bureau) predicted that digital advertisers would need to increase their spending by 30% to a whopping 200% just to maintain similar levels of ROI to previous periods.[1] For B2B brands and anyone selling something with a considered purchase, that inflation had already hit by 2021, as supply chain issues and economic turmoil left smaller markets to sell to

---

1   "IAB State of Data Initiative 2022: The Measurement Dilemma," IAB, February 8, 2022, https://www.iab.com/insights/2022-iab-state-of-data/.

but didn't reduce the number of competitors for consumer attention.[2]

And even in e-commerce industries, digital ad costs have been skyrocketing. Ads in the beauty industry have risen 41% in cost. For home and garden, it's 33%. For pet supplies, it's 27%.[3] Any market where supply costs are rising, spending is tightening, and advertisers remain focused on driving their growth on the back of digital advertising is going to continue experiencing this same inflation.

To be clear, I'm not against paid ads. Later in Chapter 9, Ryan and I will show you how to use paid strategies to jump-start traffic to content that you own and control. But on its own? Sounds like money I'll never get back.

WHAT WE SHOULD KNOW BUT DON'T

In 2015, I found myself at the helm of another business, a digital marketing analytics startup founded with one goal: to help CEOs like me better understand the actual impact of their marketing. And by 2019 or so, you could not step one foot in the marketing industry without hearing how important *content* was.

If you're reading this book, there's a good chance that the statement "content is king" is enough to make your eyes roll out of your head. It might sound trite, but what's amazing is that even

---

2   Theresa Swiggum, "Media Cost Inflation: What to Expect in 2022," Collective Measures, June 2, 2022, https://www.collectivemeasures.com/insights/media-cost-inflation-what-to-expect-in-2022.

3   Sara Lebow, "How Google's Search Ad Prices Have Risen across Retail Categories," Insider Intelligence, November 16, 2021, https://www.insiderintelligence.com/content/how-google-search-ad-prices-have-risen-across-retail-categories.

though everyone says it, and everyone claims to believe that content is central to a digital marketing strategy, no one really knows how to make it work. Every "content is king" article talks about digital transformation, meeting customers where they are, providing valuable content, and answering customers' real questions, yet many businesses continue to use the "go out and brute-force find them yourself" brand of marketing they've gotten comfortable with.

Even B2B brands that should be focusing on quality organic content have for too long focused on paid advertising, simply because that particular brute-force approach comes with data. It looks good on spreadsheets. Even if the story being told is bleak, it's more compelling than, "Well, we wrote a bunch of blogs that cost thousands of dollars and we're not really sure which of them has driven leads, if any."

But the world is changing, and with it the way people make purchases. It's also getting more sophisticated when it comes to data about *everything*. Technology is constantly offering new database structures and the ability to process more and more massive amounts of data. With every increase in customer data, it seems more like we *should* know what's effective and what isn't when it comes to organic content—but up to now, nobody has succeeded.

No matter how pretty or fancy our ads, or how many impressions we're getting, or how many people clicked on our social media post, as the CEO, my questions are always the same: Does our target market actually see and engage with our content? Are we driving qualified leads? Are we making real, quantifiable sales as a direct result of our marketing efforts? Do we even *know* the answers to these questions?

While we might have phrased the questions differently, it turns out that Ryan and I were working on the same problem. And the longer we worked on it, the more we realized we were facing the same common enemy.

CHAPTER 3

THE REAL VILLAIN: GUESSWORK

For all the sleepless nights and wasted money, we might have gone on forever without discovering a solution to our content marketing problems if it hadn't been for one watershed moment.

After his investment banking firm, Toph started a new company called DemandJump with Shawn Schwegman, the former chief technology officer (CTO) and VP of marketing at Overtstock. com. Shawn was with Overstock as they grew from $10 million to over $800 million in revenue in just five years. The fact that a CTO became VP of marketing at such a successful brand should tell you something about the importance of data to marketing in the digital world.

We founded DemandJump on the basis of that understanding: that marketing is more about making sense of the data than it's ever been before. We'll talk more about DemandJump later because that's the company where Toph and Ryan came together and created the catalyst for writing this book, but in a nutshell, DemandJump's entire purpose was to use data to make better marketing decisions.

We wanted to offer customers insight into where internet traffic came from—where competitors were getting their traffic, which websites got the most traffic related to the company's product or service, and so on—and how to leverage the data to direct that traffic toward themselves.

As part of their data testing process, the DemandJump team decided to run analytics on their own website to see how much traffic they were getting. Over the several years the company had been in existence, DemandJump marketers had written over 400 blog posts, and Toph wanted to know how many of them were driving significant traffic and qualified leads.

The answer was 4.

Out of 400 blog posts, only 4 were generating results.

For a company whose entire promise was to use data to better understand how to get more traffic, it was an unsettling discovery.

When he saw these numbers, Toph stumbled directly into the great open secret of content marketing: the waste. The reality is, only a small fraction of content ever generates any results. He already knew as a CEO that it was hard to quantify content marketing and that a lot of what was created wasn't demonstrably effective. What he hadn't realized was the massive extent of the problem.

It was at that moment that the first seeds of Pillar-Based Marketing were sewn, although we didn't know it at the time. Back then, Toph was just trying to figure out, *why is this happening?*

In order to understand Pillar-Based Marketing and why it works, you first have to understand the problem it's trying to solve. That problem is guesswork. Then, as now, guesswork was rampant throughout the entire field of content marketing.

It was the villain lurking silently in every client meeting where Ryan found himself powerless to ask for more time. It was the reason so many blogs went unread, so much organic content was useless, and so many marketers found themselves lying awake at night.

Discovering that only one percent of your content is having measurable results isn't pretty, but it was a critical moment in getting to a solution that actually works. That was when Toph first realized how disturbingly habituated everyone had become to the massive amounts of wasted time and effort in content marketing in every industry—and it's when he started asking the data scientists on his machine-learning team to figure out a better way.

RESIGNED TO THE WASTE

Don't worry; we're going to get to the solution. But first, let's parse out the problem.

The first issue is that many marketers have become comfortable with the guesswork. Or if they're not comfortable with it, exactly, they're at least resigned to thinking that's the way it has to be.

Guesswork underlies almost every step of the content marketing process, from deciding what keywords to use to choosing which pieces of content to write and how long to make them.

It's there at the very beginning of a new campaign when some-one makes a decision about what topic or theme to pursue. It's the puppetmaster pulling the strings when a marketer is led to write about their boss's domain expertise instead of something their audiences are truly hungry for. When seasoned marketers launch a new content campaign, they prepare themselves to wait 6 months for results—at a minimum. The average is closer to a year or 18 months to see if their content will garner significant traffic. And sometimes, as we discussed in Ryan's story, the only result of an SEO content campaign is the questionably helpful knowledge that whatever you tried didn't work at all.

If the only problem was that you had to wait a year to see your results, that would be bad enough, but the reality is that 90.63% of web pages and blogs get no traffic at all.[4]

Zero. None. Ever.

Whoever put in the time and effort and love to write those web-sites waited 6 months or a year or 18 months—only to realize that most of their content generated no results. That's a slightly prettier picture than DemandJump's original 1% success rate, but it's still not very attractive.

Then there's the reality of search behavior. All marketers know that ranking higher in search results is important, but do you really know how important it is? Of all the people searching for a topic, the vast majority click on a result on Page One. Half of users click on the first three results. So it's not just that you aren't getting any traffic *right now*. if your blog isn't ranking on Page

---

4   Tim Soulo, "90.63% of Content Gets No Traffic from Google. And How to Be in the Other 9.37% [New Research for 2020]," *Ahrefs Blog*, January 31, 2020, https://ahrefs.com/blog/search-traffic-study/.

One, you're probably *never* going to get potential customers clicking on your site.

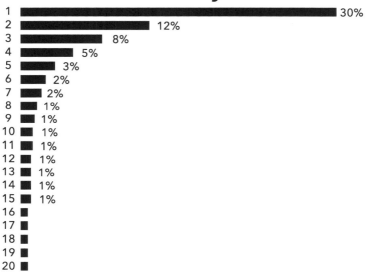

Traffic Share by Position

Position	Share
1	30%
2	12%
3	8%
4	5%
5	3%
6	2%
7	2%
8	1%
9	1%
10	1%
11	1%
12	1%
13	1%
14	1%
15	1%
16	
17	
18	
19	
20	

If You're Not On
PAGE ONE,
It Doesn't Matter

Think about it: how often do you click through to the second, third, or fourth page of search results?

How long does it take to get to Page One? The expert consensus is that it takes most pieces of content nearly two years to get there.[5] Do you have that kind of time?

And online traffic is only becoming more important. Individual customers long ago moved their product research online, but as of 2021, even 70% of B2B customers prefer digital self-serve and remote human interaction before reaching out to a salesperson or a company rep.[6] More than ever, marketers have to be able to capture that online search traffic throughout the customer journey, and capture it early—on Page One. When you consider how many different questions customers might be asking along their journey and how many topics they might search, it's easy to see why simply *paying* to be on top of Page One for every possible search that might bring customers to you is impractical at best and impossible at worst.

While many marketers may have learned to resign themselves to these realities, it's clear they're not happy about it. One in three marketers reports being anxious that they don't see immediate results from their efforts. Only 33% of marketers say they are completely satisfied with their ability to create more relevant experiences with customer data, and even among the top 15% of performers, less than half are satisfied. When they're looking for data, 75% of marketing leaders want better insight into how content is performing, while 72% want better insight into

---

5   Adam Bennett, "Why Getting on Page 1 of Google and the SERPs Takes Time," *Cube Creative* (blog), January 8, 2021, https://cubecreative.design/blog/getting-on-page-one-takes-time.

6   Arnau Bages-Amat et al., "These Eight Charts Show How COVID-19 Has Changed B2B Sales Forever," McKinsey & Company, October 14, 2020, https://www.mckinsey.com/capabilities/growth-marketing-and-sales/our-insights/these-eight-charts-show-how-covid-19-has-changed-b2b-sales-forever.

audience behavior and preferences.[7] Here we are in a data-rich world, almost drowning in information, and marketers still can't make sense of the data they have to feel like they're doing their jobs.

And with the world moving even more fully online post-COVID-19, the pressure to effectively interpret and act on all the available data is ratcheting up even higher.

THE WRONG DATA AND SO MUCH OF IT

The confusing part of all this is that there is a ton of data out there. Marketers use data every day and integrate new kinds of data whenever it becomes available—and more becomes available literally every minute.

We have access to so much information, from click-through rates to search data, sales figures, and customer surveys. We have personas that we've developed and reports from our internal domain experts. What we don't know is whether any of this information reflects, or helps us speak to, what customers are actually looking for.

More to the point, the historical tools built for marketers, including SEO tools, don't help them make sense of the data they have.

Guesswork in marketing, in other words, isn't about not having enough information. All the data in the world is nothing if you have to figure out what to do with it on your own. For every

---

7   Mike Kostow, "84% of Marketers Say Customer Expectations Are Changing Their Digital Strategy," Salesforce, August 25, 2021, https://www.salesforce.com/in/blog/2021/08/future-of-marketing-strategy.html.

individual tactic in the marketing world, there's an overabundance of available information and no way to know which of it reflects actual customer behavior and needs—or how to create content from it if we did know.

OUTDATED TOOLS

A lot of companies hear what we have to say about marketing waste and irrelevant data, and they agree. But they also think that they already have the answer: customer data.

They tell us they are doing customer surveys. After all, they say, if you want to know what customers really want or need and how they really behave, all you have to do is ask them. Or marketers and CEOs tell us: Don't worry, we're already collecting tons of data on our customers' behavior. We track them on our site. We track their responses to our emails. We have data on every single action they take from the moment they first engage with us.

Using customer data to inform your content marketing can be a good start, but in a lot of cases, customer data is another form of guesswork. In the first place, customer surveys only gather information from people who have already purchased from you. Clearly, whatever you're doing is already working for them. There's no way to know whether their behavior can tell you how to reach the potential customers you haven't connected with. And it certainly can't tell you how large the potential pool of customers is, or how many or which categories of potential customers you're missing completely.

And let's be honest. When we say customer data, we're often

referring to quantified versions of our own gut instincts, anecdotes, and experiences. Marketers often develop personas, for example, by talking to people who have interacted with customers, whether those are sales reps or domain experts. Then those personas become the ideal versions of customers, when they may or may not reflect the reality of customer needs and behaviors at all, but rather a particular person's beliefs about or history with certain memorable individuals.

Customer data is invaluable when it comes to the creative aspects of content marketing. When you know who your ideal customers are, you can train yourself to better speak their language and relate to them. But that same data is worthless if you aren't absolutely positive that the content you're choosing to write is fully representative of the search behavior of your target market.

We also know from decades of research that even if people don't outright lie on surveys (we mean this in a loving way), they often skew their answers based on what they think the person asking the question wants to hear. More often, customers don't actually know the truth themselves, or don't want to disclose it. How many of us can really say what series of convoluted search steps we went through to reach a certain web page? Who wants to admit that they found out about your restaurant because they were searching for ways to get a date?

This is the purest form of what is called data bias.

What you need isn't what customers think they remember, or what they're willing to tell you, but a move-by-move recreation of their real-time buying behavior. In a world that can increasingly offer real-time information about how customers actually behave, customer surveys and internally derived customer data are outdated tools.

SHIFTING YOUR MINDSET

By now, you're probably getting the picture. Everything we've said in this chapter comes down to one key idea: there is an abundance of data in the marketing world. But unless you know that it actually reflects customer behaviors, pains, desires, and needs and can tell you how to act on them, it means nothing.

Marketers don't have a data problem. There's tons of data out there. Too much data, actually.

What they have is a making-sense-of-the-data problem.

The result is guesswork.

Guessing which person's instincts about customer needs and behaviors is correct. Guessing which blog topics will catch customers' attention. Guessing which approach to apply.

Over many years of working with marketers, we've realized that when we don't know what customers need or want, we end up talking about ourselves. We pitch our products and how great we are, hoping that will be compelling. We talk about the keywords and topics that relate to our industry or can be tied directly to a purchase intent. We write blogs based on the personas we've developed. It feels like an evidence-based strategy because it's based on the best information we have, which is information about ourselves.

But what happens when we do this is that we write 400 blog posts and wait six months or a year only to find out that 99% of our content is dead in the water. The end result of that costly and time-intensive process is certainly more actionable data. As Ryan found in his years running his content marketing agency, the challenge was to convince clients to trust him long enough to see how real customers out on the internet would react to new content. The new content itself was a guess, but given enough time, he could learn what seemed to be most relevant to customers, which topics got the most interest, and which keywords to target moving forward.

Finding actionable data should not be that costly, in time or resources.

The end of guesswork is getting the *right* data, and the ability to make sense of that data, that will align you with real customer behaviors and needs, and getting it at the very outset of your content marketing and SEO efforts.

All the waste and uncertainty we've talked about in these first three chapters, all the sleepless nights, all the anxiety, and throwing good money after bad, suggested to us that we may have been thinking about content marketing all wrong. We needed a complete mindset shift.

Actually, two mindset shifts.

It's critical to have the right data and, more importantly, the right analytics tools to actually understand, prioritize, and decide how to use that data. But in order to know what the right data actually is, we had to pull the rug out from under the prevailing assumptions about content marketing and start over from scratch. The next two chapters take you through these two major reframes and why they are necessary if you want to understand, align with, and speak to the needs of customers in the real world.

After all, today's internet is a reflection of the human brain.

CHAPTER 4

THINK SPIDERWEBS, NOT FUNNELS

First mindset shift: it's time to throw away the funnel.

If you've been in sales or marketing for any length of time, you've heard a lot of people talk about funnels. A well-designed funnel is supposed to pull in as many people as possible at the top, and the number gets smaller at each successive level of engagement, until at the bottom of the funnel you're left with a small number of actual sales. We've even heard the concept of flipping your funnel and prioritizing the best leads that are most likely to make it to the bottom right from the start. It's a great concept because it gets us closer to the idea that keeping the bottom full means putting a lot of junk at the top. But therein lies the broader problem.

The problem with the funnel approach is that it's wasteful—requiring you to cast a huge net to catch any traffic—and it's out of touch with real-world customer buying behavior.

The internet was built to help people find products, services,

and information. It was not built to help products, services and information find customers. Misunderstanding this is the sole reason companies and marketers have struggled with digital marketing for the last three decades.

In other words, the funnel is old tech. It's from a predigital era when marketing was at best a numbers game, and there was no way to target a specific audience.

Before we talk about the infinitely better concept that will replace the funnel, let's take a moment to look at how buying really works. Imagine for a moment that your company sells boat shoes. Your first impulse might be to write content about the features of the boat shoes you sell—maybe they're waterproof and have a revolutionary nonslip sole. Unfortunately, it's not that simple.

On the one hand, you have a guy, let's call him Matt. Matt already has 15 pairs of shoes in his closet. He has hiking shoes, boots, wing tips—he's got the right shoe for every activity. And right now, he's looking to round out his collection with a good pair of summer shoes. Heck, maybe boat shoes would be good. Matt already has an image in mind of the type of shoe he wants, so he types in "boat shoe comparison" to see what's available. He clicks on a blog about different brands and options, and from there, he clicks a link to a cost comparison guide for shoes. Oops! Turns out the ones he likes the most are also the most expensive—isn't that always the way. So he switches tracks, hits the back button, and searches again, this time looking for, "Which boat shoe is the best to wear without socks?" From there, he finds a review of shoes that breathe well and work better without socks. He notices they're from the same brand as the ones he liked earlier, and he decides to go with them.

Gina, on the other hand, is looking for a gift for her husband. His birthday is coming up, and he's going on a sailing trip with his buddies, so she searches for "gift ideas for sailing trip." The results reveal a slew of gift ideas for boat enthusiasts, so she clicks on a blog post about different ideas for boat-related gifts. Most of them are for people who own boats, which aren't relevant for her, but one of the items listed is boat shoes. She's stunned. Do you have to have special shoes to get on a boat? Momentarily forgetting her husband's birthday, she heads down a totally different path, starting with, "Why can't I wear my sneakers on a boat?" Way down the rabbit hole into boating enthusiast forums, she finds a link to a blog by a boat owner complaining about shoes that slip around on deck and take forever to dry. That links to an article by two other boat owners complaining about visitors who wear shoes that mark up their boat decks. Gina notes that both these writers talk favorably about a new kind of boat shoe with a patented sole. She decides to get those shoes for her husband.

Matt's Journey

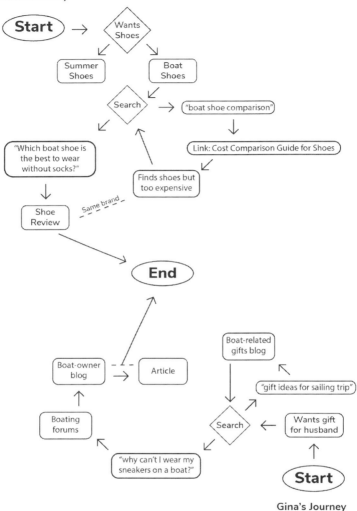

While both of these buying journeys ended in the same place, their starting points—and the routes they took to get there—couldn't have been more different.

At no point did either of these eventual purchasers actually search for the brand of shoe they ended up with. (Gina never searched for "shoes" or "boat shoes" at all.) Neither of them made the purchases they initially expected to make, and their searches, despite ending up in the exact same place, had almost nothing in common.

The point is, *buying is not a linear act*. We know this intuitively because this is how we search for things ourselves. We don't know where we'll find the solution to our problem—often, we don't know what specific solutions even exist. We're just following the breadcrumb trail until we find what we're looking for. And that solution often falls into the *I'll know it when I see it* category.

It bears repeating: at this point in its history, the internet is a reflection of the human brain.

It's complex and networked, running from one point to another along the lines of human needs and thought patterns. Once we had internet-enabled smart devices at our fingertips all the time, we stopped filtering our searches. We no longer search keywords or terms; we enter in our questions, concerns, dreams, fears, pains, and desires directly, in full sentences and multiword phrases. And then we click and scroll and hit the back button and start over in a highly complex way that looks a lot more like a three-dimensional network than a straight line.

Despite its intuitive familiarity, it's harder for marketers to get into this mindset than you might think. Would most shoe companies think it's their job to educate people about what to wear on a boat, or the etiquette of visiting someone else's boat? Or about gifts for boating enthusiasts? When you start looking more deeply into real-world search behavior, you realize you had no idea what weird, winding pathways are actually bringing people to your site. No number of marketers in a room could guess at every single pathway from an initial search to a final purchase, and even if they could predict that the Ginas of the world might be searching for boat-related gifts, why would they ever choose to focus their SEO strategy on that one pathway over others that deal more specifically with people trying to buy shoes from the start? But If you somehow *could* understand all the chaotic thoughts around a given topic and align to them, you would give your target customer ways to find you somewhere along their journey, no matter how convoluted it might be.

This became our first critical mindset shift: we stopped thinking in linear terms about how great our product is or how people might search for us and began to think instead in terms of what people are actually thinking. What pain are they trying to solve, or what desire are they trying to fulfill? And not just one or two or some of these pains and desires, but *all* of the possibilities. We started thinking in terms of networks, the circling and interconnecting lines of influence and relationship among all the topics and thoughts and questions that people were encountering.

You know: spiderwebs.

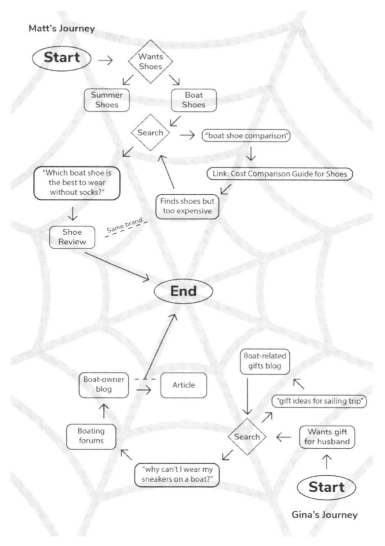

Matt's Journey

Start → Wants Shoes

Summer Shoes · Boat Shoes

Search → "boat shoe comparison"

Link: Cost Comparison Guide for Shoes

"Which boat shoe is the best to wear without socks?"

Finds shoes but too expensive

Shoe Review — Same brand

End

Boat-related gifts blog

Boat-owner blog → Article

"gift ideas for sailing trip"

Boating forums

Search ← Wants gift for husband

"why can't I wear my sneakers on a boat?"

Start

Gina's Journey

Isn't it funny how well these seemingly unrelated journeys actually fit together if you place them onto a spiderweb? Turns out, this is what search behavior looks like around any topic.

THE PROBLEM WITH FUNNELS

To see how revolutionary it is to think in terms of spiderwebs, you need to understand why funnels don't work.

In the first place, waste is built into the structure of the funnel approach. The foundation of the whole funnel concept relies on the expectation of fewer and fewer people at each level of engagement. Traditionally, a marketing campaign is designed for the top of the funnel to cast as wide a net as possible. It's built around the broadest keyword terms, with content designed to appeal to a huge audience of even remotely plausible potential customers.

To carry the "boat shoes" illustration further, the funnel approach would be to target broad terms like "boat shoes" or even "shoes" and hope that a small subset of those individuals searching want your specific type of boat shoe.

Once a potential customer is "inside" the funnel, so to speak, engaging more and more with your site and your products and services, you give them the opportunity to learn more about you, and you get to know more about them. That's when you can start to narrow the funnel and drive them toward a purchase, expecting, however, to lose most of them along the way.

After working in this way for so long, we've become resigned to the idea that the top of the funnel has to be huge because we don't know who is a potential customer and who isn't. We're resigned to the idea that you have to create tons and tons of content to cast the widest net, to bring as many people as possible to your site just in case they happen to be potential buyers.

Even our metrics reflect this reality, with their focus on impressions and page views. We're obsessed with getting as many eyeballs as possible onto this content we created and afraid to narrow our scope at all in case we lose even one visitor. As marketers trying to report progress in terms of measurable numbers to a CEO who wants to know what's working, it's natural to focus on how many visitors our website attracts. Even if the vast majority of those visitors don't care enough about what we're saying to buy anything, or leave our site after just a few seconds, at least it's something we can measure and, to some extent, predict.

The entire concept of the funnel is built on this belief—a certainty in marketing circles—that there is no way to know ahead of time what specific content will appeal to the people who will actually eventually buy our products, so we have to get as many eyes on the page as possible.

The question, then, is why can't we know which content people really want?

Remember how we said that buying isn't a linear act? It turns out that's putting it mildly.

In fact, buying is a complex, often circular, deeply individual, often emotional process that is different for each person involved, even when the "person" involved is a company and a committee, or a team does the buying.

A recent study published by Gartner® researchers proves the point. In their deep look at B2B buying behavior, they found that "virtually every B2B purchase spans six distinct 'jobs' that buyers must complete to their satisfaction to successfully complete a complex purchase: Problem identification, Solution exploration, Requirements building, Supplier selection, Validation, [and] Consensus creation."[8] Furthermore, according to Gartner, "Although these six jobs occur in each interaction, the way in which customers progress from the starting point to a purchase is unpredictable, inconsistent and sometimes repetitive. A better depiction of a B2B buying journey is likely to look like a disordered web rather than linear chevrons."[9] (As a side note, these insights apply to considered B2C purchases as well.)[10]

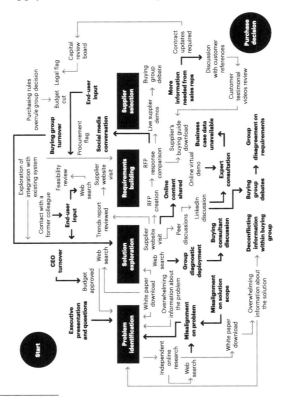

8   "The B2B Buying Journey," Gartner, accessed October 6, 2022, https://www.gartner.com/en/sales/insights/b2b-buying-journey.

9   Ibid.

10 Thank you to Heike Neumann for initially bringing this report and its critical findings to our attention.

For a closer look, scan this QR code to see the original graphic.

The tasks are predictable in the sense that every buyer goes through all the steps in one way or another, but they are neither linear nor straightforward. Each of the six represents a completely different set of questions people ask, and totally different search behaviors and search topics.

Finally, Gartner says that "90% of all buyers reported revisiting, or looping back, to at least one job as part of their overall purchasing process."[11]

With so many winding, circuitous pathways toward a purchase, you don't want to wait until someone is already searching for your specific solution before you engage with them. You want to meet them early, often, and with content relevant to each task and each question along their journey.

Remember, buying doesn't start or end with your product. It starts with pain—with a problem someone wants to solve and a set of questions they want to answer. Or it starts with a

---

[11] "The B2B Buying Journey," Gartner, accessed October 6, 2022, https://www.gartner.com/en/sales/insights/b2b-buying-journey.

desire—something they want to improve or replace. If you pick just one of the buyer's tasks and write to it, you miss valuable potential entry points into your product or solution. In general, content marketers tend to focus too much on the last two steps and overlook the much broader potential for engagement at the problem identification stage. When someone is still asking, "What am I doing wrong?" there is a whole world of opportunity to teach them about your solution that they may not be open to further along in the process.

Consider one of our customers at DemandJump who had created an entirely new method of sales forecasting.

Our research told us that a significant part of this company's addressable market was still stuck using legacy tools like Excel to handle their sales forecasting work. And they were never going to look for a new tool until they discovered that Excel was the wrong one.

In other words, it was not enough for this company to write content about what made their new technology revolutionary because a significant portion of their potential market didn't even know that such a solution existed. Counterintuitively, their best approach was to develop organic blog content around questions like "How do I generate forecasts in Excel?"—and drive customers to their better solution from there—because those were the questions the customers were searching.

We'll get into the specific details about how we would use the principles of Pillar-Based Marketing to identify the questions an innovative brand like this should be answering. For now, it's enough to know that the counterintuitive approach we recommended was both completely new to the company and exceptionally effective. It wasn't easy to convince a young company that their best bet was to write content about a competitor's product, much less about the most dominant competitor in the market. But it worked.

What was originally a stumbling block for them became a great opportunity to step in and educate clients so early in their buying process that they didn't even know they were in it.

> As a side note, this is one of two separate times Demand-Jump customers decided they needed to target the Excel brand with their organic content—and in each of these instances, those brands were able to supplant Microsoft itself as the top result for the search terms they chose to target. No small feat.

When you understand and can use the data to visualize the true complexity of the buying process, it becomes clear that the funnel approach is too linear, too narrow, too one-dimensional, and too focused on the endpoint of the buying process to reflect real buying behavior.

Instead, we need a model that looks like the behavior it represents. That model is the spiderweb.

WHAT IS A SPIDERWEB?

We're not talking here about the icky thing you run into in your attic or the stuff Peter Parker shoots out of his wrists. In marketing terms, a spiderweb is a real-time snapshot or map of all the searches a target market conducts; the questions it asks;

and how it's all related in terms of connectivity, frequency, and how far away each connectivity point is from the main topic.

Okay, that's a mouthful. Let's break it down.

Let's say you wanted to rank on Page One for the keyword term "content marketing" because you are selling a content marketing software tool. You're creating a campaign around that term, so you look at the estimated search volume for that term, opportunities to win backlinks from authoritative sites already ranking for that term, and so on. Anyway, that's what you would do with any current marketing approach. But that's thinking linearly—thinking that everyone who wants to buy a content marketing tool is searching "content marketing." Thanks to our understanding of real-world buying behavior, we know that's not the case.

Search engines also know that's not the case. Think about your own search experience. As you search, the text in the search bar autocompletes based on what it knows other people are searching. Then, once you've got results, you only have to scroll down a little to see the "people also ask" section, with a list of four or five closely related questions. Scroll to the bottom of the results page, and you get a whole section of related searches. In other words, modern search engines are already communicating, even to everyday users, the interconnected context and network of related searches. What they're showing you is a tiny snapshot in time and a tiny fraction of the total number of related terms and questions around the searched topic.

On this mock-up of a search engine results page, we see the many ways search engines provide contextual next steps to users based on their queries and the related queries of other people seeking similar information. These include the autocomplete suggestions in the search bar, as well as the "People also ask" and "Related Searches" sections.

The full spiderweb is a macro version of that: everything in the related topic's network, including not only the related terms and queries but which other terms and questions each topic is most closely related to, exactly how closely each of them is related to the others, and how often people who ask one question end up asking another. It's a complete picture of all the interconnected terms and questions in the network that tells you where your highest-value content will come from. It empowers you to write and organize content that reflects the organic, complex reality of how people are actually searching for information. The complete spiderweb represents what we call a Pillar Topic network, and it shows you not only the keywords people are searching, but how to act on that knowledge.

The difficulty for marketers, even when they've comprehended the value of the spiderweb, is figuring out how to map the network. One approach would be to enter a search and just keep clicking on related searches, then more related searches, then more searches related to those, and so on to get a better understanding of all the interrelated questions people ask around a Pillar Topic. But it would take you months to get through all the related terms for even a few keywords that way.

Similarly, you could use existing SEO tools to quantify the total search volume for a particular keyword, then identify some closely related keywords and the search volumes for those, and try to create a spreadsheet to capture the ever-expanding list. Unfortunately, we've found that a complete list of related keywords in a Pillar Topic network's spiderweb can end up being anywhere from a hundred to several thousand related terms and questions, depending on your initial topic. On top of that, a spreadsheet can't take into account how those keywords are used in questions (which is the way many people actually search), nor the traffic related to those questions.

Humans don't communicate in real life with one- to four-word keyword terms. So why do we treat communication that way in the digital world? Why do we ignore the questions people ask in plain language in favor of broad-interest keywords? One reason is that search engines don't reveal search volume estimates for questions, so a legacy tool using search engine data is likely to show a big zero next to a question, drastically underrepresenting the importance of questions to authentic customer search behavior and pushing marketers to focus on keywords that show up in the tools' dataset, whether or not they represent higher real-world volume. And when search volume for keywords is revealed, the data shows different numbers in different places, so marketers don't even know whether the data representing search volume is accurate. Nor do they know if people searching for that term represent their target market.

And even if you could account for all the questions and manage the enormous scope of the data in a given Pillar Topic's network of search behavior, you'd get at best a one-dimensional model that lists the terms without any of the connections, nodes, or frequencies of connections among them. More to the point, with any of these manual approaches, the results would be moot anyway because it would take so long to do the work that any insights you got would be outdated by the time you finished.

The spiderweb isn't just a list of terms and volumes. It is a visual diagram of the full three-dimensional, interactive, and complex relationships among all the search terms and questions contained therein. It shows every hub and spoke representing the twists, turns, and restarts that happen in the buying process. It shows how structurally important some terms are, how centrally located they are in the spiderweb, and how connected they are to other terms. As a result, the spiderweb is actionable immediately, with predictable results, because it gives you the onramps and access points to get *all* the traffic related to your topic.

That part is of critical importance. This perspective shift means you're no longer concerned solely with showing up on Page One for "content marketing" or "boat shoes," which are highly competitive and overly broad terms. It means you're instead thinking about all of the different terms people search around those topics and making content decisions based on ranking on Page One for as many of those terms as possible. It's the difference between trying to earn 20,000 clicks by putting all of your eggs in one very difficult-to-win (not to mention maintain) basket and easily earning 20,000 clicks by spreading those eggs out across all the baskets your competitors aren't even paying attention to.

The beauty here is that for a highly competitive keyword topic such as "content marketing," you can win the category over your competitors without getting on Page One for that topic phrase at all. You win it instead by owning the most important things around it that your target market actually cares about. This strategy not only gets you on Page One but directs the exact, focused traffic you want to your website and your solution.

We knew we were getting this point across when one of our customers, a Fortune 100 software company, said, "I don't care about ranking on Page One for CRM. I want to own everything that people are thinking, and asking, around it."

That is understanding the power of spiderwebs.

To get this kind of full-scale view of the system, you have to go directly to the source. You have to access the total available pool of organic search data to provide a complete three-dimensional picture, and you have to be able to do it in real time.

HOW IT WORKS

One way to understand the spiderweb concept is to think about LinkedIn or Facebook. These sites are constantly generating a dynamic network that understands how people are connected to each other across the entire universe of users. These companies have to be able to visualize, in real time and in three dimensions, which users communicate with each other and how often, which users have lots of connections and which only have a few, where there are major hubs of activity around powerful influencers, and where there are mini-hubs of a few highly engaged users around niche interests.

The content spiderweb does the same thing, using a similarly connected network (although not exactly the same math) to understand how words and concepts are connected to each other, rather than people. And, like Facebook, it shows us how those concepts connect across vast networks, how closely each node is connected to the others, what concepts lots of people are talking about and which ones only a few people relate to, and which concepts lead to others that might be closer to or farther away from the central terms you're interested in.

We're not going to get into the nitty-gritty here of how we've designed the technology required to build your spiderweb; we'll get to that in Chapter 7. But the basic process is this: You start with a core idea, a Pillar Topic, and you enter it into a machine-learning algorithm that searches it. The algorithm then uses those results to design related searches and then designs even more searches related to those, in an ever-expanding exponential web. Even with months of free time and an army of marketers, you couldn't generate this level, depth, and breadth of information with any number of manual searches and spreadsheets.

As the algorithm repeats this process over and over and over again and learns from it, it begins to see the same search questions and terms pop up again and again, more and more frequently. That's when you know you've got the complete picture, and you can visualize the entire spiderweb in a graph that shows the high-value hubs and the smaller related side streets: some with just a few small branches, some at the center of dozens of high-traffic highways.

Some terms and questions turn out to be "long tail": very specific, often multiword terms or questions that don't show up as frequently but offer insight into niche keywords you can totally own. Some topics, on the other hand, will be mega-hubs, "short tail" terms that everyone wants to own. The spiderweb can show you how to enter those big hubs from the sides—from connected branches with less competition. Or you might even see that a mega-hub is not as relevant to how people find your product as you initially believed.

For example, you might see in a spiderweb for the Pillar Topic "boat shoes" that Gina's original search of "gift ideas for a sailing trip" shows up again and again, and therefore represents a surprisingly valuable source of traffic—or at least a critical concept you have to address if you're to become an authority on the topic of boat shoes. At the same time, you might find that a more traditional, purchase-driven keyword like "organic boat shoes" isn't as big an opportunity as a bunch of marketers in a boardroom might have guessed. Cater to Gina's real need, and you can wait to tell her why your shoe is so great after you have built digital trust with her.

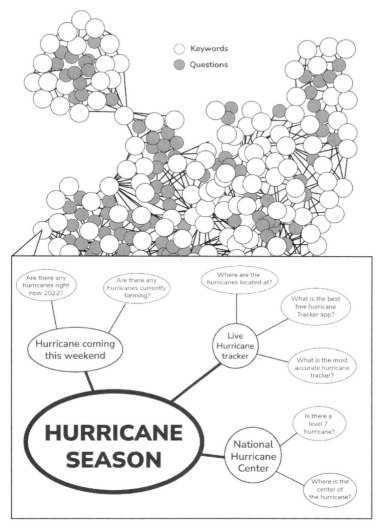

The spiderweb, which looks something like this, maps every keyword and question people search related to a Pillar Topic and shows how they fit together in a network. Thinking structurally about how people move across that spiderweb, as opposed to the individual search volume potential of any one term within it, is key to becoming an authority on a Pillar Topic and winning Page One rankings.

As a result, you understand more than the search volume, relevance, or performance of a single term—or a few terms, or even ten or a dozen terms—which is what the linear, funnel model gives you. You understand *thousands* of terms and the connections between them.

In other words, the spiderweb identifies the patterns in the data, the ways that different terms repeat themselves, and how topics branch into and connect with one another. It's a visual map of how the entire potential universe of content around your product fits together, so you can see and start prioritizing what's important and translate it into an executable strategy. It's a thing of beauty.

In the second part of this book, we'll take a closer look at how we untangle the spiderweb for a term like "hurricane season" and translate it into an actionable Pillar Strategy like this one.

More importantly, it's quantifiable, machine-learning fast, and powerfully actionable. It's a superpower that lets you optimize your content for the entire network, not just a single keyword.

HOW TO MAKE THE SHIFT

To make the shift from funnels to spiderwebs, we as marketers need to make a few key changes in how we approach content marketing and keywords. Keep in mind that to make these mindset shifts actionable, you will need technology that automates the process.

1. Start by understanding how people really talk about a topic, not just the primary keyword of the topic.

    People search for information online the same way they talk about problems in their real lives: they ask questions, seek multiple solutions, take roundabout and circuitous paths toward an answer, and go down rabbit trails away from and back toward their eventual purchase. Understanding how people are *really* talking about the topic we are interested in immediately positions us to be exponentially more aligned with, and therefore present in, their buying journey.

2. Understand not just words but whole "conversations" customers are having about the topic.

    Most of the time, when marketers have thought about SEO in the past, we've thought in terms of "short tail" phrases: one- or two-word terms that describe broad categories (such as "shoes" or "content marketing"). At the very least, we've prioritized them and put them up on a pedestal as the most important prize to be won. Just as we need to understand the many pathways that customers follow on their buying journey, we also need to understand the entire scope of the conversation around any given topic, including the pain point or problem that is the reason for the conversation in the first place.

3. Don't be the friend who tries to "jump right to the solution to the problem."

   Today, there is zero difference between how we communicate in the real world and how we expect to communicate on the internet. We use complex, long sentences and don't bother to filter or rephrase what we want to ask—and we like the content we engage with to respond in kind. Imagine that you asked me a question in person about a problem you were having, and I responded by saying, "My software that does something similar is $7.99 a month, and you can buy it now!" You would probably not want to continue that conversation. Businesses resort immediately to telling customers about their solutions because they don't know what customers are really thinking. If you ask me a question in the real world, I'm going to answer the question. I'm *not* going to say, "Guess what, I'm really awesome, and so is this product you didn't ask about." Content on the internet needs to work the same way.

4. Design content to rank on Page One for the questions customers are asking and the ways they are talking about the topic, not just Page One for the Pillar Topics (main keyword terms) you think are most valuable.

   This is the key to the entire "think spiderwebs, not funnels" mindset shift. We already know that ranking on Page One is the Holy Grail of content marketing—but we've been putting all of our efforts into ranking on Page One for those short-tail, big-budget keywords that don't match the way our customers are searching, don't encompass the entire conversation of long-tail topics around the main keyword, or are simply far too competitive to take on directly. Modern search engines see all topics as related contextually, so if you want to demonstrate the kind of authority that makes you competitive for the big terms, you *have* to rank for the related ones. It's as simple as that.

Making these shifts allows you to create and publish content on your site in a way that directly mirrors the network of searches online, aligning you directly with customer behavior and ensuring that your content appears at every step in their search, along whatever winding pathway they might travel.

WHAT HAPPENS WHEN YOU MAKE THE SHIFT

What does it look like when one of our customers starts to shift their mindset? How might your content marketing change if you started working with the whole spiderweb?

Let's look at an example.

A while ago, DemandJump was working with a customer in the life settlement industry. In case you haven't heard of it (we hadn't either), this is an industry that allows seniors to sell their unwanted or unneeded life insurance policies. When an older person with a life insurance policy either doesn't need it anymore, or needs some immediate income instead, they have traditionally been allowed to simply give up the policy and get some surrender value from the issuer. But the amount would often be miniscule. They ended up losing a lot of money, but they didn't feel like they had a lot of options—especially since continuing to pay premiums didn't make sense either.

The life settlement market offers another option. It's an investor's market in which accredited investors purchase the policies, give the owners a sum of money down, make the payments for them, and then collect on the policy when the owner dies. It sounds a bit strange to most people at first, but it can be a much better option for a senior on a fixed retirement income who needs to lower expenses, increase liquid assets, or both.

Since this industry offers a product that's pretty much exclusive to seniors, the big players have typically invested most of their marketing spend on daytime TV. But as tech-savvy baby boomers have gotten older, some of the companies have realized that they need to be online.

Our customer was in this position. For years, before we made the spiderwebs mindset shift, Ryan had worked with them in traditional funnel-campaign mode to produce content in two buckets: general lifestyle content for seniors (such as science experiments to do at home with grandkids, or creative ways to fund vacations) and content geared toward financial advisors who advise seniors (so they would know about this option for their clients). We were falling into the same traps all marketers were in: casting a huge, broad net outward to the customers we thought might be interested in the product, talking about the topics we thought those customers would care about, and hoping all this content brought some small portion of them to our client.

No matter how much content we were throwing out there, the traffic wasn't growing very much—or very fast. Yet our market research suggested that the market of both seniors and financial advisors who knew about this option was growing substantially.

Why wasn't our content connecting with this expanding, online-savvy customer base?

Simple. We weren't speaking their language.

When Ryan eventually teamed up with Toph and his company's new technology, the content spiderweb for this client revealed that the term being written about, "life settlement," was not just a term people weren't searching; it wasn't part of the conversation they were having at all!

It made for a bad Pillar Topic for the same reason that the sales forecasting customer we talked about earlier couldn't just talk about their new product. The market didn't know anything about this term—no matter how central it seemed to us.

Fortunately, unlike traditional SEO research, our spiderweb looked way beyond search volumes and clicks for our selected keyword and showed us the conversation customers actually *were* having. What people were talking about wasn't "life settlement." Rather, it was, "selling a life insurance policy," "cash surrender value of an insurance policy," and "how do I calculate the value of my policy?"

These insights not only changed our keywords but gave us a specific content strategy to make our clients the leading educators on these topics online. Our new Pillar Topic became "selling a life insurance policy," and with some manual work to sort out queries related to the job of an insurance broker, we were rewarded with a spiderweb that showed us the actual, real-world questions seniors were asking about this topic.

It was a 180-degree shift, from wide-funnel, linear thinking based on what we assumed people were interested in, to targeted, strategic content based on how the customers who wanted this service were actually talking about it. No more wasted time and effort writing random blogs about fun senior activities and hoping a small percentage of readers moved further down the funnel. And the client was able to go from trying to grab customers to educating and empowering them. It was a win for everyone.

And it really paid off; over the course of just three months, this customer went from 17 Page One keywords related to the actual conversation their prospects were having to a whopping 263.

When we first started to see these kinds of results—when we were able to shift from writing dozens of blogs and hoping a few would land to writing precisely targeted content that we knew would plug into real customers' conversations—we were almost afraid to believe it. But then we saw it work for customer after customer after customer, across all kinds of domains and industries and every size and structure of business.

That's the power of the spiderweb.

THE DATA OUTSIDE YOUR FOUR WALLS

By this point, it should be clear that content has to align with customers' buying behavior in order to be effective, and to align with customers' behavior, we have to talk the same way they are searching.

The problem that many companies encounter, though, is that they don't even know the field they're playing in. To put it another way, we as content marketers tend to take internal directives about marketing and create content to project them outward, rather than following what the target market actually is thinking and aligning to that. This critical mindset shift is what will enable you to start looking at the entire market and seeing how much of it you can own.

Seeing this play out over and over with our clients led us to realize we had to combine the spiderweb approach with another shift in our thinking: to stop valuing what we do know and start focusing instead on what we don't. Because the data inside your four walls can never compete, in objectivity or scope or power, with the entire universe of data outside your four walls.

CHAPTER 5

THINK OUTSIDE, NOT INSIDE

To understand the second mindset shift, we need to start with a question: are you letting your internal goals set your marketing strategy, or is it based on an objective understanding of the market you are trying to approach? In other words, are you driving your strategy from the data inside your four walls, or from data about the actual market that exists outside them?

Being able to see the spiderweb—the entire network of connections and back alleys along the customer buying journey—gives us enormous insight into how to align with customers around the topics they are talking about. But it can also show us that there is a whole universe of potential market activity of which we're not even aware. We start to see that the methods we've been using to create content strategies, from instinct to domain expertise to customer data, aren't giving us anything like a complete picture.

The reason for that is simple. All of our approaches to understanding customers are really about us, us, us.

Take lipstick, for example.

On the one hand, let's say you've got a cosmetics company focused on organic ingredients. They've done strategy sessions and market research, and the CEO is positive that their differentiator, their unique market value, is their organic product. Their research shows that the organic product market overlaps a lot with vegetarians, so she directs the marketing team to generate a keyword list of the terms related to vegetarians and the other products they buy. The marketing team gets to work creating content and placing paid ads on related websites, like a popular juicing blog and a site that showcases organic grocery stores.

One of their competitors, on the other hand, is a legacy brand, a well-known name in cosmetics with a long history. The CEO of this brand prides himself on the brand's extensive variety of styles, from traditional matte and glossy looks to new glitter and metallic shades. Rather than keyword data, this company relies on customer feedback from surveys on their website, focus groups, and even talking directly with customers in stores. Whatever they hear from these customers, that's what they write about.

These two companies represent the two current state-of-the-art approaches to discovering what content to create. One is data-driven, compiling lists of keywords and search volumes and getting information on cross-marketable industries. The other is customer-focused, spending most of the marketing budget on getting information directly from the people who buy their product.

And though they're coming at it from two different perspectives, they are both making exactly the same mistake: making internal assumptions about what they think matters, taking internal sales goals, determining how much traffic they would need to meet those goals, and then trying this and that approach to reach those goals. There's no pressure on them to figure out the size of the entire market they could be addressing because their goals are all driven internally—hitting certain sales numbers based on the sales funnel, in particular. There's no pressure to look for information outside the data they're already gathering, whether it's keyword data or customer surveys.

As a result, they're at a standstill. They're getting as many customers as they can get using their respective approaches. They're gathering valid data and writing good content, and yet neither of them is making substantial gains in traffic.

That's because neither of these companies is aware of the most powerful question their target market is asking. More about that in a bit.

Focusing internally on our own goals, and the information we already have, will never show us the true size of the market we could be capturing. Internally generated information is biased, arbitrary, and extremely limited. Even within an individual company, one person's keyword list looks very different from another's, and each person's interpretation of which customer survey results to focus on is different from everyone else's. And while internal data can give us more insight on what we're already doing, it can't show us the vast universe of potential outside the limits of our current thinking.

We can't use information we already have to expand into the

universe of potential customers we're not already addressing. We can't even know how many potential customers there actually are.

When it comes to organic content, nobody has ever understood the actual size of the prize. What we think the market is, based on our internal goals and information, and what the real world looks like are two completely different things.

THE SIZE OF THE PRIZE

You might have heard the acronyms TAM, SAM, and SOM.

At first, it sounds kind of like that trigonometry rhyme we all learned to remember sines and cosines (remember SOH-CAH-TOA?). In fact, it represents a set of common metrics that businesses use to understand the size of their potential market—and a level of visibility into the whole universe of customers that content marketing should aspire to.

In order to attract investors, a fledgling business has to prove that there's a market. No matter what their product or service, no matter how great it sounds on paper, they have to be able to prove that there are a certain number of individuals or businesses interested in, able to afford, and likely to purchase it. TAM, SAM, and SOM refer to the "total available market," the "serviceable available market," and the "serviceable obtainable market."

To put it succinctly, these three measures tell you: (1) how much actual demand there is for the proposed product or service, (2) the segment of the market that's within your actual reach (that you can "service" effectively), and (3) the portion of that total market that you can reasonably expect to capture. Together, they create a quick, broad-scope, quantifiable picture of "the size of the total prize" your business can target.

More than ever, content marketers need their own version of this.

Instead of focusing on internal goals and internally focused information, marketers need to develop an objective metric for understanding:

- the total addressable market for their content in terms of traffic;
- how much traffic they are actually driving, relative to that available total; and
- what they need to do to drive more of it.

Historically, organic content just hasn't had that kind of measurability.

The shift that needs to happen is to understand the "size of the prize" available to us. Not the sales goal the VP generated this quarter. Not what our existing customers tell us they want more of. Not how many searches have been conducted recently on a best-guess list of keywords we generated in a brainstorming session. We need an objective, complete picture of the entire possible addressable market—a version of the TAM, SAM, and SOM numbers, but for traffic. One that hasn't been achievable before the technology and best practices of Pillar-Based Marketing.

Once you know the size of the total prize, you can also see how much of the total you're getting compared to your competitors, where they're getting parts of it you haven't even addressed, and which parts of it you can own.

This is insanely good news for marketers. Marketing leaders in every company are expected to participate in the numbers that drive the business forward, to show how marketing contributes to what matters to the CEO and the board. Historically, it's been easy to arrive at internal targets for marketers based on sales and revenue goals, but that leaves marketing trying to drive an organic strategy based not on the actual number of customers or what they are talking about but on arbitrary internal concerns. It's a double bind because reaching those internal goals is necessary to keep their jobs in the short term, but focusing on them keeps them from achieving the full potential of marketing for top-line business goals like revenue growth and new business generation. It's the same problem growing startups run into when they build their sales-hiring plans around an arbitrary number they're trying to reach rather than backing into what is actually achievable by starting with the SOM and setting goals according to industry benchmarks.

That's the dog chasing its tail, with the marketer running in circles trying one approach after another to meet arbitrary numbers.

Having an objective, complete picture of the size of the prize allows the marketing leader to turn this process on its head. It makes organic traffic just as understandable and knowable a thing as the total market the business is going after.

WHAT CAN I OWN?

Knowing the total addressable market for your content also helps you prioritize. It lets you figure out which part of the market you can own. Rather than selecting a keyword or topic internally and trying to rank with it, you can select an area of existing customer interest and write directly to it, with full confidence that you know both what to write and how much of the total traffic you can expect to own by doing so.

For example, if you had access to the real-world search data around the Pillar Topic of "lipstick," you could learn a lot from the specific search volume numbers surrounding each of the long-tail terms people search about lipstick. You might find topics to cover that you never imagined were being searched, like "lipstick is made of pig fat" (which, for the record, is a real term of very high value in the "lipstick" spiderweb and could play very nicely into the strategy of the organic manufacturer). If you could add to that a deep knowledge of your competitors' SEO rankings, you could prioritize developing content around the niche questions customers are asking that your competition is not answering at all.

Like everyone else, marketers live with the reality of limitations. There aren't unlimited hours in the day or writers on the staff or dollars in the budget. If you had unlimited budget and time, you'd write everything. Right? Actually, that's funnel thinking again, hoping that creating more and more content across a broader and broader set of topics would eventually lead to "down-funnel" sales.

One of the two biggest reasons companies fail is that they're not focused enough on something they can crush in a specific segment of the market, and marketing has the same problem. If you could "slice and dice" the market you play in and the size of the prize for each of the different potential content strategy variations, you could be laser-beam focused on aligning to one specific target market. But if you don't know what the target is, you can't do that. So instead, you try something based on a guess or on internal data, and when that fails, you try something else.

This is how marketers develop shiny-object syndrome. It's why funnels are still so popular. We're trying to be everything to everybody instead of *knowing* the exact right content to write for the specific customer we want to align with.

We think: we have some customers who care primarily about the ingredients in our cosmetics, so let's build a content funnel for them around that. Other customers are focused on value, so that's the funnel we'll build for them. And so on.

What if, instead, you could sit back at command central and see, holistically and unbiased, what the whole universe of your targetable market really looks like—the real world of the customer, the product, and the market as a whole? You might not like what you see at first. It might show you that there's a lot of market you're not addressing at all, or that your competitors are killing it in areas where you're not even competing. You might discover that you've been wasting hundreds of hours on biased, incomplete data and that the analysis you've been making is so limited that you don't even know what you're missing. You might see that your picture of your industry and your customers is not like the real world at all.

There's a reason no one wanted Galileo looking through that

telescope. Realizing the world you've been living and working in is only a tiny fraction of the whole picture is disconcerting. Our first response is often to want to ignore or deny it.

BUT.

That kind of holistic picture, as little as you might like it at first, gives you a power that you could never have otherwise. You can hold in your hand a model of the entire universe surrounding your product or service, see nodes of conversation and interest that were invisible to you before, select a single, knowable target, and create exactly the right content that lets you own that piece of the field.

In the end, wouldn't it be better to know the subfield you could own, and then fully own it, than to keep guessing how to get into the arena at all?

HOW IT WORKS

When a new company sets out to define the market they're in, they have one significant advantage over content marketers: a "market" is something you can objectively define. You can quantify it. A market is the total number of people who are interested in, or could be interested in, purchasing a particular product or service. It's a concept that the business world is familiar with, and all a company has to do is gather the data.

Content marketers are dealing with something more ambiguous: a "topic."

In the previous chapter, we outlined the process for developing what we think of as your Pillar Topic's spiderweb: the complex, interconnected network that shows how people are searching for and talking about your topic in the real world. But what is a topic? Is it a word or phrase that describes what we sell? The issue we think our customers are most interested in? A question that's come up multiple times in customer feedback? The term with the highest search volume? Or the one the CEO likes best based on her experience in the field?

Using any of these internal measures leaves the concept of "the topic" in the realm of the murky and the subjective. It's why there's often so much argument about which topics or keywords are the most relevant to our marketing. Everyone has an opinion.

We determined that you can take something as fuzzy, gray, and undefined as "a topic" and define exactly what that topic looks like on the internet. You can take the whole concept of topics outside the realm of guessing and hoping and make it *objective*.

Let's look at our lipstick example again. When we look at the entire spiderweb for "lipstick," we see some terms that we'd expect people to be searching for, but with the added value of knowing the specific language that's most commonly used, such as:

- What are the most popular lipsticks?
- Best everyday lipstick
- Which lipstick brand is best and cheap?

What we also get, though, is a whole list of terms that tell the story of human interest around the topic of lipstick, topics that few marketers would prioritize or even dream of developing content around, like:

- History of lipstick timeline
- First lipstick brand in the world
- Lipstick was invented to simulate
- Why was red lipstick popular in the '40s?

These terms are all more than mere curiosities in the broader spiderweb surrounding this Pillar Topic. The technology in DemandJump's platform is able to contextualize each search term based on how frequently it shows up in the countless journeys customers take while searching for lipstick. So we also know that these terms are some of the most common, most fundamental, and therefore most valuable. If a brand wants search engines to see it as an authority on "lipstick," it needs to develop content around these terms.

That is how you build digital trust and outmaneuver your competition no matter what industry you're in.

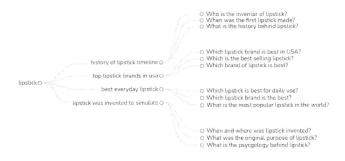

In case you happen to be in the lipstick business, here's a sneak peek at some of the actual top keywords and questions people search around the topic.

It makes sense to us as marketers that we can measure something like advertising spend. You have a campaign with a certain number of creative assets that cost a certain amount to develop, a certain number of dollars that can be spent, a certain number of bids received, and so on. All of that is very objective and quantifiable, so that's where we end up placing our trust. But none of that tells us anything about the total available traffic for our content, which the spiderweb does by showing the complete picture of everyone who is talking about, around, and in relation to a specific topic from any angle or perspective, not just from the keyword phrases you've pulled data for. Maybe it can tell us how well we're optimizing for a search engine, but we're not trying to optimize for search engines—or we shouldn't be. We should be optimizing for customer experience, or what we like to call SXO, a much more powerful approach than SEO for driving results.[12]

As content marketers, we're trying to do something beyond selling a product to a defined market. We are trying to create content to match experiences. We are trying to create a content universe on our own site that mirrors and reflects and takes on the same shape and texture as the complex network of human interactions that is the search process.

And how do you objectively measure experiences?

To a lot of people, measuring experiences or perceptions seems more like pseudoscience. It doesn't seem like something that can be objectively understood. Before the smartphone, they might have been right, but now that people are integrating

---

12   Thanks to Adam Helweh for his insight on this, which you can hear on our podcast, *Page One or Bust!*

search into every action and decision throughout their day, we have unprecedented access to unfiltered, raw, straight-from-the-human-brain search data. Data that captures in real time the billions of internet-enabled devices responding to the impulsive, unfiltered questions, concerns, and needs of billions of individuals every day. All the information exists, but before now, we lacked the ability to look at it properly.

Until recently, the sheer complexity and size of the data has made analyzing it impossible. Because the internet reflects and resembles the human brain, linking across surprising and unpredictable connections and creating previously nonexistent networks, mapping a topic has been as apparently out of reach as mapping a thought.

That's what we came to understand working on the problem of quantifying content marketing at DemandJump, and that's why we designed a machine-learning process that works like a brain. It's based on neuroscience and trained to map the entire universe of experiences and thoughts hidden in search data patterns, not from the starting point of our assumptions but objectively and in full.

Thinking outside, not inside, is about applying that data to objectively measure the totality of experiences and perspectives that define a topic. Put another way, this mindset shift is about redefining what a "topic" is: it's not a keyword term you want to tell people about but the universe of interrelated thoughts and experiences that real people are having, which over time centers naturally around a particular phrase or question they innately and intuitively use to search for what they want.

And *that* becomes your Pillar Topic, the central topic that holds up the entirety of your organic content strategy.

HOW TO MAKE THE SHIFT

In the past, everything we've done as marketers has been based on internal data about existing customers, not a picture of the entire market or potential market. We were thinking about domain expertise, not customer alignment.

The key to making the shift is to let go of your biases, your assumptions, and what you think you know about the market you're in. Don't let your experience with customers in the past taint your perception of the current or future size of the total available market.

1. Don't think about your product, value proposition, or domain expertise, but rather what the data says customers are actually thinking about.

   This sounds a lot like what we talked about in Chapter 4, but it goes even further. The spiderweb is a way of expanding outward from your topic to ensure that you're capturing all the related content. Using the "outside" data is about defining the topic in the first place. Instead of starting where we've always started—with our needs or goals as a company—we need to start by looking at the entire picture of what people on the internet are talking about. In Chapter 7, we'll talk specifically about how to compare the many potential Pillar Topics you *could* write about and choose the one with the most opportunity to tackle first. To do that, we need to look outside. It's like sitting in a meeting, and instead of wondering what people want, you open the window and listen to all the people passing by. They probably aren't talking about you, but you'll quickly learn what they do care about. When you start talking about those things, they will listen.

2. Don't limit yourself to what you already know about your customers.

    As marketers, we often pride ourselves on how much we know about our customers. We're often the customer experts, reporting on surveys and market research to help our colleagues understand what customers want. To create content that drives exponential Page One rankings, traffic, leads, and customer growth, we can't continue to do what we've always done. We need to put our egos aside and be open to knowledge we don't have, which often includes everything our customers are talking and thinking and dreaming about that's not us. When we are open to the objective data about what customers care about, we can create content that connects with them intuitively, immediately, and powerfully. It also builds digital trust.

3. Instead, learn the size of the prize and allow that broader data set to drive your decisions.

    One thing we hear from marketing leaders all the time is that they want a seat at the table. They want to drive real business growth and make marketing critical to the company's bottom line. They want marketing to be part of the company's strategy, not an afterthought or a check-the-box exercise. That requires aligning marketing with how businesses measure success, which is to first determine the size of the total available market (or the total available traffic, for marketers) and base your decisions on how much of that market you can reasonably expect to capture. Thinking outside, not inside, doesn't simply align marketers with customers. It aligns them with CEOs, boards, and other business leaders. It's your ticket to a seat at the table. And while Pillar-Based Marketing starts with your organic content strategy, it creates insights for your entire marketing program that can drive true product-market fit. Imagine now that the results of your work are making it into board meetings—becoming key strategies the CEO is sharing with investors. Or if you are delivering these results as an agency, your work is now making its way all the way to your clients' board meetings. If that isn't a seat at the table, we don't know what is.

WHAT HAPPENS WHEN YOU MAKE THE SHIFT

What do we talk about when we talk about lipstick?

Let's return for just a moment to the two companies from the beginning of this chapter. Based on their internally focused decision-making processes, one company directed all of its content marketing toward vegetarians and others interested in the "organic" market. The other company wrote content about its wide variety of product styles, including its traditional and contemporary lines.

Neither company's content made much headway.

To understand why not, we have to expand our view. We have to zoom way out to our complete, "outside" picture. Not the picture of how people talk about our products, or what kinds of products they want to buy, but the picture of what people are thinking and worrying and asking about, and therefore searching for, when they think about lipstick.

When we zoom out, we see that what people care about most in their lipstick isn't whether it's matte or shiny or organic or anything else about the lipstick itself. We shared some real examples of important questions and phrases people are searching around the Pillar Topic of "lipstick," but we didn't share the single most important question people ask.

The most commonly searched question about lipstick is:

"What does lipstick stand for?"

What people want to know is, what does my lipstick *mean*? What does it convey to others when I wear this color or that color? What types are appropriate to wear to different events? What is the significance of each lipstick choice I could make? Why should I care about lipstick at all, for that matter? Who says I even need to wear lipstick?

When you think about it, that makes sense. Lipstick isn't just a haphazard purchase. Wearing lipstick isn't just about how I think I look. It's about sending messages, communicating with others, being part of a social interaction. It's about choosing to either participate in or buck beauty standards that have long, complicated histories. It's tied up with all kinds of other emotions and insecurities and identity issues that thoughtful consumers wrestle with every day. It's about what it means to wear lipstick, not just what it looks like.

So while these companies are building their SEO lists, and their marketers are arguing about topics to write about and trying to justify their choices and waiting six months or more with crossed fingers hoping they're driving enough traffic, they could have skipped the line and gone straight to the top of the rankings if they'd owned the one question lipstick buyers really care about. A question that guesswork would never have led them to answer.

Everything not related to the concerns that consumers reveal through the honest input of an internet search is wasted effort.

Until you look outside your four walls at the complete, real-world picture in the data, you can't possibly hope to know what those issues are. And you can't afford to keep guessing or hope you find it by luck.

PAGE ONE FOR THE NETWORK

Both of the mindset shifts we've discussed have one key point in common: they're about optimizing for the total network of customer behavior and customer need, not just optimizing for individual keywords. The behavior you care about, the behavior you want to influence, happens in a network along the strange connections of the spiderweb. It's not a bunch of unrelated phrases.

Digital success today requires an understanding of the total collection of keywords, questions, and searches around any given topic and how to use those to align to what your target market and customers are thinking. Overcomplicated spreadsheets, lists of keywords, domain expertise, and prioritizing specific short-tail keywords are all ways to be a part of the 90.63% of web pages and blogs that get zero traffic. Period.

When we tell people about these two mindset shifts, even though they agree with us, they often don't believe it can be done.

They don't believe it's possible to know the size of the prize in content marketing. To be 90% successful rather than 90% wasteful. To know precisely and ahead of time exactly what piece of the market to aim for, how to write content guaranteed to own it, and how to cut past the competition to rank on Page One, not only for a specific keyword but for an entire network of interconnected topics, questions, and terms.

In short, they don't believe it's possible to make organic content and SEO strategy as objective, measurable, and profitable as any other element of modern marketing—or even moreso.

It is possible.

It is possible for you—whether you are an internal marketer or an agency.

It is possible for your company—whatever your industry or the size of your market.

We know because we've done it. Again and again. For customer after customer. In industry after industry.

Pillar-Based Marketing is how.

CHAPTER 6

THE BIRTH OF PILLAR-BASED MARKETING

April 19, 2019. The date is etched in Toph's memory because it's the day everything changed.

That was the day his team posted a blog to their website called "What is a good CAC?" It was a pretty typical blog post: a few hundred words of text and a couple of graphics. There were no banners or streamers. Nobody promoted the event on social media. There was no paid traffic. They just wrote this article about Customer Acquisition Cost using the two mindset shifts we discussed in the previous chapters and posted it on their own site.

If you don't know what CAC is, this might not seem like a big deal—and that's kind of the point. A blog on this kind of specific question is relevant to the people who care about it but not very interesting to anyone else.

What was different about this one was what happened next.

Within thirty days, it ranked number one on Page One.

It stayed within the first three results for nearly three years, without a single change, edit, or dollar of paid promotion.

As of the writing of this book, more than three years since it was posted, that blog still ranks number two on Page One for its title phrase, without anyone touching it once that entire time.

If you're in marketing, you understand why this felt to Toph like seeing the New World, or taking the first step on the moon. It wasn't possible, but it was happening. He pushed his team to write a few more articles using the same approach, driven by the two mindset shifts we've already discussed. Every single one of them got similar results.

Within a few months, they found themselves on Page One for over 100 highly competitive phrases. The further they went with it, the more they thought, "This can't be possible." But it kept happening.

So there it is, the billion-dollar question: what if you could write just one blog that would rank in the top three positions in the search results for over three years, without touching or editing or updating it once?

Or what if you could write a few dozen pieces of content and rank on Page One for over 100 competitive phrases related to your business?

What if you could *own* a whole topic that customers really care about?

It's okay if you don't believe it right now. We didn't believe it at first either. The CAC blog was our first big win, the test that made us think, "This is everything we've been looking for." But it wasn't until we saw it work over and over and over again that we started to accept that it was real.

So how did we get here? How did we do this thing that we didn't believe could be done—that no one believed could be done?

How did we crack the content marketing code?

COULD WE APPLY THIS TO CONTENT?

We didn't discover the secret overnight. It took four years of hard work and millions of dollars of applying this math to other marketing problems before we discovered how it applied to content.

Before Ryan and Toph even met, before the CAC article, Toph's company, DemandJump, was already working with internet data to help companies visualize and use networks of websites around the products and services they sold. In his mind, marketers didn't need just another marketing or SEO tool. They needed a central data hub where all the marketing data would go, with a platform that could bubble up and distill the actionable information they needed to do their jobs more efficiently.

So DemandJump was using its data analytics engine to target two things: helping companies understand how traffic was driven to their competitors (and how to divert that traffic to themselves), and showing them which websites were most relevant to their products if they wanted to place display ads.

For example, if you were selling customer success software or coffee cups, you wouldn't want to place your ads on any random site. You'd want to place them on the websites that put you in the best position to sell more software or coffee cups. When people are in the research, evaluation, or decision mode of buying software or a coffee cup, what sites are they on? That's what DemandJump was working on.

One day in a team meeting, talking about paid search, someone asked, in an offhand way, "Could we apply this to content? Could we use this data, these networks we're building and analyzing, to direct customers to write about topics that will put them in a better position to rank on search engines?"

At the time, it was a crazy concept. But it was also a very appealing concept because content marketing had nothing like this. No one was effectively using data to drive Page One rankings. Hundreds of unseen blogs on DemandJump's own website were the proof. So Toph told the team to go ahead and create a proof of concept.

That was the CAC blog.

One of their internal marketers wrote the blog. The actual content he wrote was based on search data that showed them how other words and terms were related to the central concept of Customer Acquisition Cost: the first version of the spiderweb we described in Chapter 4. The DemandJump team that worked on the blog never talked about what they personally thought they should write about, what keywords they thought were important, or their experience with customers who had CAC questions. Instead, they went straight to the data and wrote the article using the words, phrases, and interconnected topics and questions that real-world users were actually searching.

They added no backlinks. No paid traffic. They just posted it up on their own website to see what would happen.

The result was almost immediate. They couldn't believe it. They had discovered the content marketing world's biggest breakthrough. If you applied all this search data, the full spiderweb, to creating content, you could skip straight to the top of the rankings. No six-month or year-long waiting period to see if it got noticed. Just tapping straight into the neural network of the internet to align directly with the way customers are really talking.

What Toph didn't know at the time was whether he could grow the process enough to make it sellable. In the first place, the proof-of-concept math had been run manually, which would be far too slow to use for client companies in real time. And in the second place, Toph wasn't at all sure he could find a writer, or rather a team of writers, who would embrace this kind of network thinking to fuel the art of content writing at scale and build a full marketing methodology around it.

KISMET

When the CAC blog hit the number one spot on Page One and stayed there, Toph knew this new approach was important. He directed his team to write a few more articles, and then a few more, and they kept seeing similar results.

So he made a huge decision: he decided to shift the entire focus of the company to productizing this content approach, to focus on this problem that had never been solved. That year, they put thousands of hours into perfecting the math, building and rebuilding their algorithms and data analytics to be able to do it at scale.

Tentatively, he began to approach some marketing agencies, telling them, "We discovered something, and we want you to try this with your clients." But most of them were still approaching content in the old way, and even when they saw the data, they wouldn't take the leap. They wouldn't write content based on what the data was telling them; it was just too foreign to what they knew and were used to.

So DemandJump kept getting better and better at the math, and better and better at visualizing the spiderweb and the network, and looking for someone who would apply it.

The final pieces of the puzzle came together at an event for the Indianapolis tech community, held by an organization named Powderkeg.

Toph's team went to a Powderkeg event on February 27, 2020 (that's the date Ryan remembers as the one that changed everything) to announce the gold they'd discovered in the data. As it turned out, Ryan's agency, Metonymy Media, was also there, as a sponsor, looking to write content for SaaS and tech companies. Toph was looking for a partner who truly understood content marketing to execute on his data, and at the same time, Ryan and his team were writing content for big clients and becoming increasingly convinced that they needed better data. Ryan was at Powderkeg because he believed the tech industry would be where he would find the kinds of clients he needed, the ones who were willing to try new things and take the time to watch content marketing work.

It was kismet.

While hundreds of startup founders, investors, teams, and vendors networked in the dim light of the Vogue Theater in Indianapolis, Ryan and his team found themselves sitting a few feet from Toph's partner, Shawn. They got to talking.

Shawn told Ryan about overnight Page One rankings and a desire to prove the tech at scale.

Ryan wasn't convinced right away. "If what you're saying is true, it's amazing, but I don't buy it," he said. "I've seen too many silver bullets that don't work, and there are no shortcuts to quality content."

Afterward, though, Shawn went to Toph and said that he'd found their first content agency partner. He told Toph, "We need to work with them."

THE MOST COMPETITIVE KEYWORD IN THE WORLD

Once we started working together, everything sped up.

At the beginning, we were still thinking of what we were doing as writing blogs and having those blogs perform better individually. But as we wrote more of them, we started to think about a series of blogs tied together, different lengths of content tied together and addressing different needs or different subtopics in the network. The mindset shifts we described earlier in the book started to take shape as we experimented with new ways to capitalize on and make sense of the data.

The idea of the content pillar or topic cluster was starting to emerge in the marketing world at the time, and it made sense, at least on paper. If you could link articles together in a kind of "hub and spokes" model, with related articles coming together to form a mini-wiki on a certain topic, that might be a good user experience. Maybe even one that search engines would reward.

That was the context behind the conversation when Ryan and Shawn met to review the kinds of insights that were coming from the DemandJump platform. It took about five minutes for Ryan to see how understanding the whole spiderweb around a given topic could fuel something like the pillar strategy approach that was gaining traction across the marketing community. The concept of the "content pillar" that was making its way through the marketing community was just a starting point, a framework to begin translating our understanding of the content spiderweb into an actual content strategy—the strategy we now call Pillar-Based Marketing.

To test the concept and the relationship between Ryan's creative agency and Toph's technology company, we went after some central "big ticket" keywords in marketing itself, starting with "marketing attribution." This was a natural first Pillar Topic for us since, at the time, our product was still focused on marketing attribution (since then, we've shifted our focus to SEO Pillar and Pillar-Based Marketing). We created our first set of interconnected posts around this concept, with Ryan and the team at Metonymy Media writing all the content based on the data and visualizations from Toph's data platform at DemandJump.

We went from nowhere to Page One in 60 days.

Within those 60 days, as we slowly published articles one after another, we became number one and number two on Page One for this term—and also for all kinds of related search terms, including long-tail or offshoot terms Ryan would have never thought to recommend as priorities for a new client like DemandJump. To put that in perspective, we went from having no content on this topic to outranking Salesforce, one of the largest, most powerful, most prolific content writers and marketing organizations in the world.

It's worth noting that we weren't the only people thinking about this problem. The notion that you should have a focus point for your messaging, that marketers needed to get better at answering the questions people ask, was in the air. Marketing as a whole was beginning to understand that in order to rank, you needed to be more aligned with customers, to let the data tell you what to talk about.

But no one else had figured out how to do it.

When we saw the results from the first few tests, we started expanding our content, writing six or eight blogs at a time, working on the network piecemeal, building it up one piece at a time. We'd write a few posts, and then, when those shot up to the top of the search rankings, we'd write a few more.

We went on testing and testing and testing over four or five months, and we kept getting the same results—nearly immediate rankings on Page One whenever we wrote what the data told us to write. So we decided to try the ultimate test. We would go for the one, single, individually most coveted and big-ticket keyword in our world: "content marketing."

It was such a competitive keyword that, even with all the amazing results we'd been getting, we weren't sure it would work. When you try to rank for the keyword "content marketing," who are you competing against? Other content marketers, who are using their content marketing skills to rank for a term in their own area of expertise. We were literally pitting our process head-to-head against the best practitioners of all the old ways of doing this.

We even considered backing out, thinking maybe the competition was too steep. We're talking not just Salesforce but HubSpot. Semrush. Content Marketing Institute. Multiple huge entities and appropriately respected authorities that were competing at the time for all the terms in the topic network we were hoping to rank for.

Because of the massive competition, we decided to go big. Instead of writing one post, and then another, and then a few more, we wrote 89 blogs of varying lengths and published them all at once, using an interlinking strategy designed to resemble the spiderweb we found in the data. We wrote 89 because that was the number the data suggested we needed if we wanted to be truly authoritative on the subject, and if we'd learned anything, it was to trust what the data were telling us.

Of course, this was a big investment in terms of time and

resources, but don't worry; we're not saying that you have to write this amount of content at once to be successful. We were trying to win some of the most competitive keywords that exist, and that was going to take serious firepower. Most topics don't require anywhere near this level of initial push. In fact, as you'll see in later chapters, we have come to believe that with just 16 pieces of content, any brand can realize the kinds of immediate organic rankings that prove the concept of Pillar-Based Marketing and justify further investment in the strategy.

The day came when we had our content ready, and we pushed "publish."

Even with all the months of previous wins, even with our belief in our data and our content-writing ability, the results were astounding.

Within a matter of weeks, we were getting dozens of rankings we wouldn't have gotten any other way. We weren't just ranking for the single keyword "content marketing" but for dozens of questions, keyword strings, and subtopics related to content marketing. We were dominating the network.

Top 100 Keyword Rank Trends

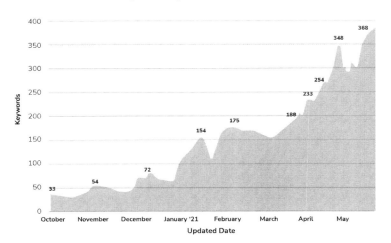

Page One Keyword Rank Trends

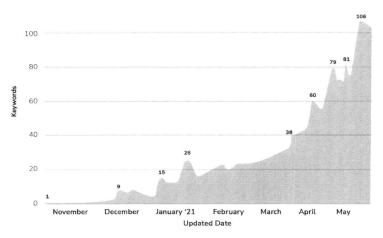

This is a chart displaying the number of keywords within the "content marketing" spiderweb for which DemandJump ranked (a) on the first ten pages of search results and (b) specifically on Page One before, during, and after publishing our initial wave of 89 pieces of content.

That's when we started going to our customers with our newly minted strategy and saying, "You need this."

It's important to remember, too, that this wasn't an isolated incident. Ryan began baking this approach into his work for every one of Metonymy Media's clients, and DemandJump began packaging Ryan's services in with their own customers who loved the promise of the data but were far from ready to invest all the in-house resources it would take to implement the strategy. As we started getting customers to test the process, we got to apply it in industry after industry, and we saw the same results in every case: when we went after a topic with this strategy, at a minimum, we got on Page One, and almost always in the top three, within a matter of weeks, sometimes within 24 hours.

We even saw salespeople on customers' teams writing blogs for topics like "medical wire rope," landing on Page One in a matter of days and staying there to this day with no changes.

At the time of this writing, DemandJump alone currently holds 791 Page One rankings for keywords and topics in our "content marketing" pillar, with 82 in the very top position—and the list grows daily. Right now, we aren't on Page One for the term "content marketing" itself, but we are one Page One for hundreds of related terms, which means hundreds of different intersections with customers at different stages of different buying journeys. If anything, we've proved that what matters in terms of measurable results is the aggregate presence we can build across the entire spiderweb. Reach and specificity are what make Pillar-Based Marketing a transparent, profitable marketing strategy; striving to make it to Page One for any one term in a vacuum is vanity and little else.

It's worth saying again that these kinds of results happened for all our customers, whether they were in software, healthcare, education, B2C, baby clothes, manufacturing, whatever. They could be selling five-gallon buckets; it didn't matter. In every case, they overtook their competitors in a matter of weeks or less. It became a common occurrence for us to check in on rankings mere *hours* after publishing new content for a customer and find them on Page One.

We'd eliminated the waste. The anxiety. The guesswork. We could finally predict ahead of time exactly what content would rank for real customers in the network.

ENTER PILLAR-BASED MARKETING: THE ONLY APPRECIATING ASSET IN MARKETING

While we were testing and experimenting, seeing the results, and bringing more and more customers on board, we needed a way to talk about what we were creating. The more we built the methodology, the more we realized that we weren't just building onto existing SEO or content methods; we were creating an entirely new marketing category, or at the very least, a sub-category that enables and empowers marketers to drive a level of success in organic content that they have not previously experienced.

That was the birth of Pillar-Based Marketing.

In a nutshell, Pillar-Based Marketing (PBM) is quantifiable organic alignment to customer behavior.

This is the opposite of the "build it and they will come" mentality Toph talked about in Chapter 2. When the internet first existed, everyone took the "build it and they will come" approach. And then paid search was invented. You could bid on keywords and brute-force pay your way to success over people who didn't have as much money, and you could win easily.

But we've arrived at a point in the history of the internet, and the sophistication of internet users, where that doesn't work anymore—and not just because search engines are starting to charge an arm and a leg for people trying to brute-force their way with paid ads and weak organic alignment to customer behavior. At this point, being authentic and aligned to actual customer behavior, the actual search journey, is the most important foundation for digital success. As we've said before, more than 90% of blogs get zero traffic because they're not aligned to the behavior of the target market.

So you end up paying to get traffic. And paying, and paying some more. Organic content doesn't work that way. Effective organic content is evergreen. Once you make that first investment, you don't have to keep making it over and over again. It's an asset you own that ends up being more and more valuable over time, whereas paid search becomes more and more expensive over time.

Yes, you will have to maintain your content, and you will even produce more content to support your growing Pillar Topic networks as you see the results, but the organic leads you get in B2B and, in B2C, the new customers you get while spending no pass-through money to do it, will delight your CEO. And for the PLG freemium and free-trial companies out there, you will see significant increases in new signups.

Don't believe us? Just look at the exponential increase in DemandJump's marketing-qualified leads (MQLs) gained directly from organic content driven by PBM.

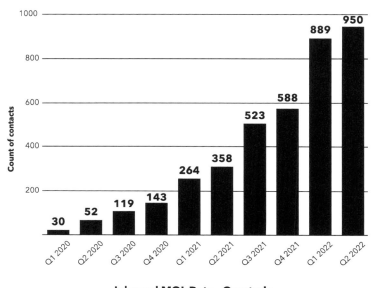

Inbound MQL Date - Quarterly

If this isn't the Holy Grail of organic content, we don't know what is.

In other words, content that actually aligns with customer needs, that gets traffic organically, is the only appreciating asset in marketing. If you can write one blog that answers a question customers care about, you don't have to touch it again for months or even years. It will continue to rank on Page One and bring in new readers and customers forever, without laying out another dollar.

PBM is the set of specific data-driven tactics that aligns your organic content with the entire network of actual customer search and buying behavior to create an appreciating asset your company actually owns and controls—now and for as long as you want.

THREE LAYERS DEEP

To drive that kind of evergreen organic content, you can't just talk about a main keyword or a single phrase. You have to become the recognized expert (dare we say thought leader?) on an entire concept, and you do that by developing Pillar Topics and building them several layers deep.

There's already lots of talk in content marketing about pillars. It's a term that is sometimes used to mean the same thing as a "topic," and sometimes refers to how an individual content creator might define their brand on a channel (like Instagram or YouTube).

What we mean when we talk about Pillar Topics is more substantial than that, more central to your actual work as a company. In PBM, a Pillar Topic is the name of a category or product or service that is, and defines, whatever is most important to the growth of your business. There are multiple Pillar Topics in every business, usually including at least one or two that act as the short description of your main categories, products, or services.

When you know what your real core Pillar Topic is, you can write what we call the Pillar Page, the core piece of content that serves as a hub for all the content on your website that's related to that pillar topic. The Pillar Page is the longest, richest, most detailed piece of content. It's called a Pillar Page because it's the central structure holding up your messaging.

PBM works a bit like a "hub and spoke" model, although it's bigger and broader and more complex than that. Once you have your Pillar Page, you build out Sub-Pillar Pages that cover related, longer-tail, more specific topics. For example, if your Pillar Topic is "content marketing," you would write a Pillar Page on content marketing itself, and then surround it with shorter Sub-Pillar Pages on topics like "content marketing examples," "content marketing types," and so on.

From there, you expand outward even further, out into the long tails of the network, writing very specific Supporting Blogs of only a few hundred words each on very specific individual questions, such as "What should I pay for a content marketing agency?"

content marketing

Content Marketing Strategy

- What are the steps of content marketing?
- What are the essential elements of a content marketing strategy?
- How do you plan a content marketing strategy?

Types of Content Marketing

- What are the different types of content?
- Which type of content marketing drives the most leads?
- How do I decide on which type of content marketing to do?

Best Content Marketing Examples

- What is the best marketing content?
- What are some early examples of content marketing?
- What is an example of content marketing?

Remember how we talked about visualizing the entire network, the spiderweb of interrelated questions, topics, and ideas that people were talking about around your topic? PBM is how you recreate that network, or a portion of that network, on your website, making your site reflect and mirror the exact shape and structure of the network of search behavior in the real world. The result is that the world—and the search engines—perceive you as the absolute experts on this topic. You're answering the questions searchers are really asking, and therefore you are providing real value to users of the search engine. You're signaling to the world that you're an actual authority on this topic. You're not just trying to rank with one keyword or game the system with a single repeated phrase.

That's what search engines ultimately value and promote. They've proven it with each iterative algorithm update since Panda, including 2022's "Helpful Content" update from Google that prioritizes content that's designed to align to actual customer or user behavior and answer real questions rather than just rank high for a keyword.

It just makes sense. Search engines have one critical deliverable—user experience. That means helping people use their search engine to find the best and most relevant content based on the terms and questions they enter. Search engines care about the user experience, not your product or service. You can talk about yourself when users discover your website.

Going three layers deep, with long-form, in-depth Pillar Page content supported by midlength Sub-Pillars and short-form Supporting Blogs on detailed topics, makes you immediately the expert on any topic that you've chosen to own. We're so committed to this approach that we use it ourselves; it's how a small company like DemandJump consistently ranks number one or number two for the ultracompetitive term "SEO pillar," ahead of all the 800-pound gorillas in the marketing industry.

NO MORE BLANK SCREEN

We've talked a lot in this book about the data and about using the data to understand the network of search behavior around your topic. But you also have to have writers who will take that information and create compelling content around it. You need the art as well as the science.

When we started working together, marrying the data with content, we were concerned that the writers might feel stifled. That they might resent the data telling them what to do. Nothing could have been further from the truth.

Instead, the writers went through a transformation. They found themselves wasting less time, expending less energy and anxiety on what to write about. We were able to give them a much clearer set of assignments and show them exactly how their work fit into the larger strategy and the bigger picture of the search network. For the first time, they could see the whole plan and their part in it. And best of all, they could feel confident from the very beginning that what they were writing was relevant and would work.

We provided them not only the keywords or topics, but specific titles that would align with questions customers were asking. We were able to look at other titles, topics, and keywords most closely related to what they were writing about so that they could pull from, talk to, and connect with that larger set of concerns. We could say to a writer, "If you're going to answer this question, here are the other questions people are asking that are related to it."

In the old system, they sat in front of the blank page and tried to figure out what to write about. Now, they don't have to waste time with guesswork and haphazard research. They can create effective content quickly, with the feeling that their writing will be a success.

Is it a challenge sometimes to align your content to what the data says? Absolutely. But our writers have learned to operate within the PBM methodology to dig deep into the data, get creative with their implementation of it, and write exceptional content on any subject matter.

PBM marries the two parts: the data and the content. The science and the art. At DemandJump, the data provides the writers the information and framework to be successful. The writers are empowered to write great content that they know will be seen by thousands, even millions, of people their customers want to reach.

The point is that PBM doesn't just work better to get you on Page One. It takes away the frustration and stress that have always come with trying to do excellent work in the content marketing space. It makes strategists, creatives, and marketing leaders happier and more productive. It's a system that builds success for everyone.

THE FIVE STEPS OF PILLAR-BASED MARKETING

So here we are. The moment of truth. Rubber meets the road. Down to brass tacks. Whichever metaphor works for you, this is where we finally tell you how it's done.

We'll get into the details of each step, with examples and specific actions to take, in the next five chapters. The good news, as you will discover, is that DemandJump has automated the process of building spiderwebs and informing exactly what content to write. For now, here are the five key steps of PBM:

1. **Choose your first Pillar Topic.**

    This step is where you challenge your assumptions about the

most important topic to write about and the Pillar that will give you the most impact for your business. You identify your first Pillar Topic by visualizing the entire spiderweb and reflecting on your business goals. This isn't as simple as it sounds because we often find that the "topic" a company thinks they want to own isn't the one the search data recommends. With real data on the "size of the prize" for each potential version of your Pillar Topic, you can see how the market is talking about each one and the effort it might take to rank on Page One for one version versus another. In this step, you will evaluate data around multiple versions of the same Pillar Topic, or even multiple potential Pillar Topics, then select the one to start with that will capture the most leads and customers in the shortest time.

2. **Build your Pillar Strategy.**

Once you've chosen a Pillar Topic to begin with, you select the most important network of related topics (Sub-Pillars) you wish to include that support the main topic. A Pillar isn't just a single topic; it includes all the related, interconnected subtopics and long-tail phrases you can find in that topic's spiderweb. This step is where you understand all the topics you'll need to write about to mirror the real-world network of search behavior on your website.

3. **Create your Pillar, Sub-Pillar, and Supporting Blog Content.**

Get ready in this step to forget everything you think you know about SEO and trust the network instead. The spiderweb of Pillar and Sub-Pillar Topics that you built in steps one and two become your guiding principles as you think critically not about checking keyword boxes but making sure your content is going to be valuable for the customer, and that it's better than what your competitor has. This step is where you write your actual content, including Supporting Blog posts to target very niche, long-tail keyword phrases, based on the network strategy of your selected Pillar Topic.

4. **Publish your Pillar Content.**

   Recreating the network means both writing the right content and linking all the content together on your site to mirror the buying, reading, and searching journey of your target customers. How you publish content, the order and timing and interlinking of it, affects your rankings and your readership just as much as the content itself. This step is where you start to post your content and use targeted paid strategies to kick-start the organic engine.

5. **Measure your impact.**

   A new approach requires new measurements and metrics. You'll no longer be focusing on impressions or clicks, but on how many relevant keywords you rank for, how high you rank for each of them, and how long it takes to rank. As you get more and more information, you continue to revise existing content and write new content to maximize the value of your network. Ranking data lets you see exactly which keywords, Pillars, and pieces of content are driving traffic and how important each keyword or Sub-Pillar is to your overall strategy. This step is where you can finally go to your CEO and prove quantifiably that your efforts are impacting the business.

BECOME BULLETPROOF

If you take these as your guiding principles and make PBM the core of your content strategy, it will change your life. It will become a superpower you can use to leap over the competition in a single bound. (Sorry, we had to go there. It's still true, though. Just check out the G2 reviews!)

But don't take our word for it. Here's what it looked like as we started to integrate PBM into the work we were doing with all of our clients, across every industry and size of business:

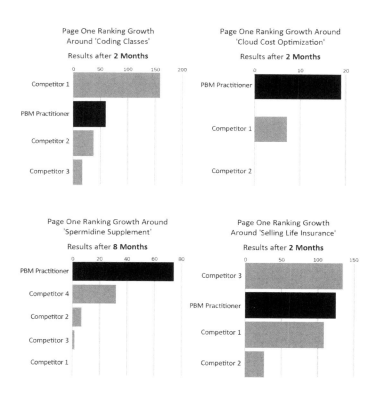

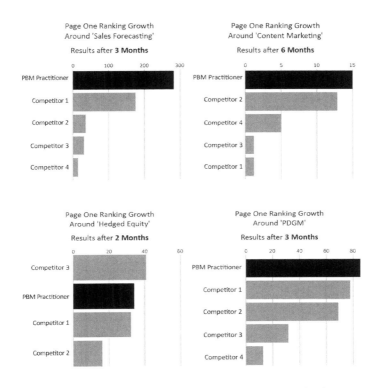

Each of these charts displays the number of keywords ranking on Page One for companies using PBM, within each respective Pillar Topic's spiderweb.

As we worked with these companies, we found that their industry and product didn't matter, nor did the size or lack of content or internet presence. It didn't matter if a company even had a blog at all before we got to work. None of it mattered. All we had to do was follow these five steps, and they got the results. We worked with small startups, all the way to Fortune 100 companies, and it was always the same.

The impact was so profound and powerful that we decided to get married. DemandJump acquired Metonymy Media in 2021, and PBM became the core of what we do. Neither of us could have imagined that a marketing technology company would want to acquire a small boutique content marketing agency, and Toph certainly wouldn't have believed he would devote his company to content marketing. But we can't imagine a better outcome from all the sleepless nights, all the anxiety, all the waste and guesswork and lack of confidence that we'd both been experiencing for years.

We knew that every marketer and CEO out there in the world was having the same problems and seeking this solution, so we decided to share it. That's what we're going to do in the next five chapters. We're very excited about it.

Just a warning, though. This is going to work so well, so fast, that it will feel like cheating. It's not. It's showing you how to truly, authentically align to and talk about what your customers care about. That's not cheating. That's just good business.

Pillar-Based Marketing has become the most critical foundational component for every company's most efficient and effective go-to-market strategy. Here's how it's done.

SECTION TWO

HOW TO DO PILLAR-BASED MARKETING

CHAPTER 7

CHOOSING YOUR FIRST PILLAR TOPIC

So far in this book, we've talked a lot about Pillar-Based Marketing, why it works, and how we got here in the first place. Now we're going to show *you* how to do it.

The first step in the PBM approach, as in any content marketing strategy, is one that seems like it should be simple but has historically been shrouded in guesswork, arguments, and anxiety: choosing a topic to write about. Out of all the thousands of possible topics in your industry, and out of the hundreds of keywords, questions, and issues that relate to your own product or service, knowing which one to address first can be surprisingly nerve-racking. Up to now, with no way to know which single topic will generate traffic or rankings, the tendency has been to throw a bunch of content at the wall trying everything at once and hoping something sticks.

PBM changes all of that. It also shows why trying to address every possible topic at once will never get you the rankings you want, and why you need to choose one core topic to address first.

Consider Jennifer. Jennifer is the CMO at EasySigner Documents. EasySigner is a venture-backed SaaS (software-as-a-service) company that's looking to grow quickly. Their main product is an online platform for securely generating, sharing, and signing documents. The company's leadership has done their homework. They understand the market niche they are in and how their product addresses a specific need of that niche. Jennifer has been assigned the critical task of building visibility for the new product to drive qualified traffic, leads, and customers to achieve the company's desired growth. She's smart, savvy, and committed, and she knows that organic content will be the critical piece of her strategy. After all, the one-and-done strategy based on ads just doesn't cut it anymore.

Jennifer has seen some success with her approach, but nowhere near the kind of traffic she needs to promote the growth rate the CEO is looking for. She's developed a few use cases for the product and written blogs around each of them. She's targeted some broad, short-tail keywords and used a legacy SEO tool to generate a list of related terms around them. She's built an editorial calendar that has her team publishing two pieces of content each week, focusing on growing each of their key topics equally over the next few months. She's even got a list of questions that the sales team says are frequently asked by customers. Everyone in the company knows they have a great product and that people should buy it. Without a better strategy to guide her, she's keeping her team focused on "netting the whales": the broad, product-related keywords with large search volumes and tons of competition.

This afternoon, Jennifer is scheduled to meet with the CEO, and she's not happy about what she has to report. It's the end of the first quarter of the campaign, and out of the 25 or so pieces of content they've put out, only one has hit Page Two on the search results, and none of the others are ranking as high as that. Altogether, her results amount to a few dozen clicks a month for the top performing blog and sporadic hits from the others. She's going to have to convince the CEO to give her more time, maybe even more money, to keep publishing a few pieces a week and seeing what works. And she knows that the CEO is going to push her to drive more qualified traffic and leads by creating more content like the piece that reached Page Two, even though she's not sure that's their best bet.

In other words, Jennifer is like every marketing leader we know—and all the marketers we've been sympathizing with in this book so far. She's doing literally everything she's been taught to do. She's hedging her bets by going after lots of keywords, and she's focusing on the biggest, broadest keywords that relate to her company's product. She's looking at search volume and gathering data on which pieces are performing. Her team is writing incredible content about the wonderful features and value her solution offers. But it just isn't driving any results.

If you've been following along with us on our journey, you should be starting to understand why this approach will never get Jennifer substantially better, or faster, results than the ones she's getting now. Organic content will never be the growth driver EasySigner needs it to be, using these outdated approaches.

In this chapter and the ones that follow, we're going to walk you through exactly what you—and marketing leaders like Jennifer—need to do instead, step by step.

It starts with putting aside your gut feelings about the need to address every audience, and instead picking *one* core topic and putting whatever resources you have into making your company the world expert on that one topic. Sure, after you totally own this one topic, you'll expand out to new ones. You won't abandon any potentially relevant topic forever; you'll just choose one to focus on first and own it completely before you move on.

But how do you know which topic to pick? If you're going to put the others aside for now, how do you decide? How do you know which one will drive the most traffic, engagement, and growth—and in particular, how can you be certain enough to feel good about doubling down on one topic instead of hedging your bets?

Let's find out.

THE FUNDAMENTALS

The first and most fundamental element of Pillar-Based Marketing, and the starting point for answering the questions above, is the Pillar Topic. We briefly addressed the Pillar Topic concept in Chapter 6, but let's define it more carefully here.

A Pillar Topic is a content topic represented by a short-tail keyword for which an organization wants to rank on Page One of search results. Pillar Topics are broad and represent the greatest opportunity for increased qualified traffic among other more specific keywords that may be related. In other words, your Pillar Topic is the arena you choose to play in, the single topic that holds up and coalesces the network of organic content you're going to build. Even with PBM best practices, you may not immediately win a spot on Page One for your chosen Pillar Topic keyword—but you will own a considerable portion of the market for the highest-quality organic traffic around that topic.

You might think that focusing on a single core topic in your marketing would be as obvious as focusing on a single core product for your startup. But in our experience working with hundreds of marketers, it rarely happens. Even companies that successfully define and pursue a single product or service offering often neglect to apply the same strategy to their content marketing. There are so many different keywords, terms, and concepts surrounding any given product or service that it's been almost impossible to know which one to choose. And because it hasn't been possible to know ahead of time which Pillar Topic would perform best, companies have either spread out to "cover their bases" or constantly switched tactics as they got new information. Neither of these approaches will work.

Consider a brand like Nike, for example. Nike's marketing department has literally thousands of potential keywords to choose from, including shoes, running shoes, apparel, sports, sports apparel, athletics, and athletic shoes, among many, many more. Setting aside their insanely high domain authority, if they were to start their organic strategy from scratch and try to write about all of these topics equally or switch rapidly from one to another, it would be a long, uphill climb to be seen as an authority, or rank high on search results, for any of them.

Jennifer's SaaS company, EasySigner, faces a similar dilemma. Customers looking for a better solution for their document-signing needs might search for any one of a number of terms, such as documents, signature, signature software, sign a document online, remote signature, e-signature, document signing, and so on. The traditional wisdom suggests that she should attempt to cover all of these potential avenues for connection, either in multiple pieces of content or all stuffed into a single piece that ends up reading like a phone book of keyword terms.

Just think about how many businesses establish a set of categories for their blog content, then develop an editorial calendar that has them producing content in each of the categories in rotation. This has been a fairly standard way of operating a corporate blog for years.

Most marketers today are aware of the importance of understanding and aligning with customer needs and behaviors, but too often, we believe we should try to do this with five or six (or more!) different topics at once. We're also making the fatal mistake of believing that the content that drives traffic on one topic will also drive traffic on others.

These are rational assumptions. But they are assumptions we don't have to make.

Choosing a single Pillar Topic creates guardrails for your organic content strategy. When you select a Pillar Topic, you are making a commitment to better understand what your customers are thinking about *this one topic* and the network of search behavior around it. Focusing in this way makes it possible to fully understand not just the topic but everything related to it and how people in the real world engage with that topic through search. This is goal one.

PBM IN ACTION

Choosing your first Pillar Topic requires three key steps:

- Build a short list
- Compare topics
- Plant your flag

Remember, you're not choosing one topic at the expense of all other topics for all time. You're choosing the single most impactful topic to address first, the topic that will drive the most qualified traffic, the traffic that will gain you the most business the fastest. Your first Pillar Topic, in other words, is the topic that offers the greatest opportunity for you right now, above all others.

However, you don't start the process by selecting a single topic. You start at the opposite end, expanding your list of possible topics by considering the spiderweb of search behavior around many potential Pillar Topics and applying the "think outside, not inside" concept to determine which one presents the strongest opportunity as a starting point.

For example, when we first wanted to drive traffic for topics around how to write content, we compared and analyzed several topics, including Content, Content Marketing, Content Strategy, Content Execution, SEO, and SEO Pillar, among others.

We chose to plant our flag first with Content Marketing for two main reasons: the size of the prize (how many people were searching for that core term), and how competitive that term was on search engines. The data showed us that many of our prospects were searching for this term and that we were likely to be able to own a large portion of that traffic.

The steps below will show you how to choose your own first, most powerful Pillar Topic.

STEP ONE: BUILD A SHORT LIST

The starting point for choosing your first Pillar Topic is to create a list of all the potential topics you could address with your content. During this step, you will generate a list of all the potential keywords, audiences, and topics related to your topic, with a focus on what customers are actually looking for—terms they are already searching.

Consider this step a brainstorming exercise, and try to step outside your existing assumptions and mindsets about your product or the market you're in. Generate as many topics and keywords as possible, including those that are related to the pain points your customers have that aren't specific to your product. You'll be analyzing the network of searches around each of the items on the list, so the more ideas you can generate initially, the more data you can gather, and the more options you'll have to compare.

Keep in mind that the Pillar Topic with the highest return may be surprisingly far outside the range of terms you've already considered. In our experience, companies have the greatest success with this process when they take the time to generate a broad, comprehensive initial list.

As you generate your list, consider the following questions.

1. **What keywords and topics have you already targeted?**

   The easiest place to start is with topics you've already considered. Look at your customer avatars, your use cases, and your product lines. Consider any information your sales team has provided around frequent questions and the industries or customers they have the most success selling to.

2. **What information is on your website, and how is it organized?**

   Include on your list all the topics that your website addresses, both the central product-oriented topics and the smaller, niche topics. How are these topics related? What larger concerns are reflected in your website's existing structure? Add to your list any topics or questions that your website hierarchy suggests are important to your customers.

3. **Do you reach some specific industries more than others?**

   Your highest-potential Pillar Topic may be more closely aligned with an industry you want to sell to than with your product per se. Think about not only how your product serves that industry but what other topics members of that industry are talking about amongst themselves. What key-words are trending in those industries that you might latch on to?

4. **What are all the pain points you are solving?**

It's easy to become overfocused on your product's features and benefits. But remember the financial services example we covered in Chapter 6: helping customers create financial forecasts in Excel (the customers' current pain point) turned out to be the highest leverage content for a company whose ultimate goal was to move customers away from Excel alto-gether. Gather any keywords, topic phrases, or questions related to these pain points.

5. **What is the one pain point you would most like to solve?**

Building on the previous point, have a discussion around what single pain point you would most like to solve for your customers. Do you want to make payroll simpler? Speed the recruiting process? Provide better insights from medical data? Force yourself to drill down on the one problem you want to solve, and include any related terms on your list.

6. **What are your business goals and objectives?**

Consider the answers to the five questions above in light of your short-term business goals and objectives. Is there a new market you're planning to enter? Is one of your prod-ucts or services sold at a higher margin than others? Think about the end results you're hoping to achieve, and be clear about which of your potential Pillar Topics are most in line with where you want to go. That could end up breaking a tie between two good options, or it could narrow your list when it comes time to make the final call.

PBM IN PRACTICE

Let's check in with Jennifer at EasySigner. Jennifer has two key product lines she knows she needs to support with her content: electronic signatures and document generation. She also checks in with sales and finds out that they are focusing heavily in two industries, namely financial services and insurance. Right away, she has a list of six potential Pillar Topics:

- Electronic signature
- Document generation
- Electronic signature for financial services
- Electronic signature for insurance
- Document generation for financial services
- Document generation for insurance

She could create a much longer list, depending on her business goals and the other information she gathers. But she chooses these six to start with because they represent her company's core areas of potential business. She wants to know which of the six topics represents the greatest potential to generate significant traffic and potentially take business from competitors. In other words, she wants to know which one should be her first Pillar Topic. **We will be following the highlights of Jennifer's search for her first Pillar Topic. For a detailed walk-through of Jennifer's decision-making process, go to DemandJump University by creating an account at DemandJump.com.**

You will know your list is nearing completion when you seek out new answers to these questions and start seeing the same topics and terms come up again and again. At that point, you've probably identified most of the important terms. If you see any terms or topics that you deem very low priority or too hard to address, you can take them off the list, but be wary of taking many items off at this point. The longer and more complete the list, the more likely you are to find that one high-potential Pillar Topic.

STEP TWO: COMPARE TOPICS

Once you have generated your list, the next step is to prioritize it. Comparing your topics is one of the most critical steps in the process and includes three different elements: understanding the complete network or spiderweb around each of your potential topics, identifying the search volume for the entire network, and evaluating where you currently rank for each term compared to your competitors. This process allows you to choose and stick with a single Pillar Topic with absolute confidence.

The prioritization step is also where Pillar-Based Marketing begins to differ substantially from any previous approach. Before, you might have tried to prioritize various keywords based on hearsay from your sales team, domain expertise from your leadership, results from paid search, or your own gut instincts. With PBM, you will be able to prioritize based on real data about the size of the potential prize and the current competitive market for each keyword or topic.

We will go through each of the elements of comparing topics below.

Understand the Network of Topics and Questions
Remember "think spiderwebs, not funnels"? This step is where

the spiderweb comes into its own. Prioritizing your list requires understanding the whole network, the full picture of all the different questions people ask, and all the topics they search around each of the topic keywords you've listed.

> Prioritizing potential Pillar Topics is not just about frequency; it's about intersections, interconnectedness, the connectivity of words to one another, and which ones are closest to the core Pillar Topic in the network.

Traditional SEO based on keyword frequency treats keywords like boxes. Each keyword is a box of a certain size. Some boxes are big, in the sense that they have high search frequencies. Other boxes are smaller, or less often searched. Prioritizing based on search frequency is like choosing one box and hoping to get all the searches that are inside it. The problem is, you don't know how people ended up in each box. If you don't know *why* so many people searched for box A instead of box B, you don't know how to address their needs. More importantly, you don't know how, or whether, any of the boxes are connected to each other—or to you, your product, or your website. You don't know whether someone who searches for a specific term ever ends up in *your* box, or if they do, how they got there.

The internet just doesn't work that way. It's not a collection of discrete, disconnected boxes. It's a vastly interconnected neural network. Looking at any one specific box can't tell you anything about how to understand or influence the behavior of that network.

Instead of seeing search terms as boxes, PBM visualizes the whole network of terms like a transportation system—a map of main streets and back alleys and superhighways.

Think about how large commercial businesses like Best Buy or Walmart choose their physical locations. They tend to be on main roads, right off big highways, accessible to as many people as possible from as many different initial starting points as possible. They can't just build a big parking lot in front of their door that's not connected to anything. It has to be fed by as many side streets and connector roads as possible.

You want the same thing for your content: to build it on a hub that's at the intersection point of as many different ways people search for your topic as possible. And you want to have signposts for your content at every minor intersection and side street where your potential customers are already driving around looking for answers.

In network, or spiderweb, terms, prioritizing each potential Pillar Topic requires you to know the following things:

1. **How many other keywords are related to, or searched with, the specific topic or keyword you are evaluating.**

   Knowing whether your potential Pillar Topic is a hub requires understanding how many other topics, keywords, and questions it connects to. When people search the topic keyword you are interested in, what else are they searching? The more ways that people connect to the keyword of interest, the more ways there are for people to find you if you own that keyword. A good Pillar Topic is a term that sits at the intersection of a lot of different searches—a term that people reach from a lot of different directions.

2. **How many other networks the topic you are evaluating is connected to, and what they are.**

    Similarly, a strong Pillar Topic keyword or term is one that connects to other kinds of networks, not just within its own network. For example, a topic that's often searched when people are looking for a product like yours is great, but a topic that ends up being searched by people who are looking for solutions across a variety of different industries is even better. Think of it like that friend who has lots of other friends. If they have a lot of friends with the same interests, they can introduce you to people who already care about the things you care about. But if they also have a lot of friends with other interests, you can get new people into your favorite activities. It's the same with search networks: you want to get new people into your network from as many directions as you can.

3. **How often people arrive at your site or product via this topic's network.**

    It's not enough for a topic or keyword to be at a central "superhighway" hub; it has to be a highway that gets them to your doorstep. If millions of people search a term, but none of them end up eventually searching for a product or solution like yours, that term might not reflect your best Pillar Topic. If your friend knows a lot of people but never brings any of them to meet you, you don't benefit much from their connections.

However you get the data—whatever strategies or tools you use—you must generate a complete picture of the complexity of these interrelationships, including all the ways people go from smaller topics to your broader topic and from their initial searches to your content.

When choosing a tool to help you, it is critical to choose one that is designed for building networks—not just counting keywords, searches, or traffic. The fact is that this process has to be automated. There's no manual way to achieve this level of complexity by downloading data in a spreadsheet. The whole point of this step is to generate the map of the network, and the only way to achieve that is to analyze literally every keyword on your list several layers deep, which means that your final spiderweb could potentially include thousands of keywords, terms, topics, and questions. If you do it right, the process is exponential, reaching out to include the network around your terms, terms related to those terms, more terms related to them, and so on until the network is complete.

> From here on out, we're going to be referencing the DemandJump platform when providing instructions for building PBM strategies and executing on them. For example, for Jennifer to begin analyzing the actual spiderweb of interconnected keywords and questions for each of her potential Pillar Topics, all she needs to do is enter them one at a time into DemandJump. The platform then goes and automatically maps the entire network around each one, providing deep insights into behavior surrounding each in a matter of just a few minutes. It's that kind of efficiency that makes this data-driven approach to organic content possible.

DemandJump's platform, to our knowledge, is the only one built to do exactly this work, to automate the generation of this network map. There are other AI content tools that train their algorithms on internet content, which includes the 90.63% of content that is irrelevant. DemandJump takes the complete opposite approach and looks at the data that is entered by actual humans derived from their brains, down their arms, through their fingertips, onto a keyboard, and into the internet. Using machine learning, the DemandJump platform constructs the three-dimensional network of hubs and spokes in real time, and it does so automatically in a matter of minutes. You could start gaining similar insight by searching your terms and all the terms you could identify that were related to them and so on, but as we've said before, this would take you literally months— and the final picture would not include the third dimension of how the terms are related to each other. It would still be showing you a list of boxes, not a map of the intersections.

Only by producing the spiderweb can you identify the location of your highest potential terms. Because a high-priority term isn't just one that a lot of people happen to have searched for. It's one that sits at the center of a hub of activity that is proven to lead people to you—or that could be leading people to you, if you had the right content.

Identify Search Volume for the Entire Network

> Once you have visualized the network, the second step in prioritizing your topic list is to identify the search volumes across the entire network. Although search volume is not sufficient on its own, getting a sense of the search volume across the entire network will add another layer of sophistication to your topic prioritization.

Keep in mind, the term or topic with the highest search volume is not necessarily the winner. The key is to use the understanding gained from the network map, plus an understanding of your business goals, to narrow your list to the one topic with the highest potential for impact.

There's no need, in this step, to get a readout of search volumes for each of your hundreds or thousands of generated terms. Rather, the goal is to compare search volumes across topics, to see which of your potential Pillar Topics' spiderwebs of keywords and questions has the highest collective volume. At this point, because you already know where the "hubs" are in your network, you can compare search volumes for those hubs and see the size of the potential prize for each. The critical point in this step is to compare how much potential traffic could be gained by selecting each of the terms you've identified.

Here again, work to put aside your assumptions. A topic you or your team thought was interesting might have a relatively small volume compared to a topic you never considered before generating the spiderweb map. And even a topic that sits at a major hub, in the sense of being connected to a lot of smaller questions or terms, might not have very high search volume compared to other hub terms.

What you will see during this process is that a few terms will start to stand out: terms that are similar in search volume, represent your niche in the market, *and* show up as hubs on the spiderweb. With each step, your list should be diminishing to include only those terms.

Evaluate Your Current Rankings

The final step in prioritizing your topic list is to evaluate where you are currently ranking with each item on the small list of high-value terms you've identified. Understanding where you—and your competitors—rank on each of your potential Pillar Topics provides a big-picture view and shows you where you can make the most headway.

One of the most common ways that companies fail to follow the mindset of "looking outside, not inside," is by focusing on what they want to talk about rather than where they rank in the currently existing market for keywords and questions. Starting from internal organizational assumptions leads many companies to use weak keywords, particularly companies that are trying to create a new category or subcategory in a particular industry—which includes a lot of SaaS companies. The temptation is to talk about the new phrase, product, or service they have created and try to generate buzz and interest around that phrase. Unfortunately, as we discussed in earlier chapters, that's not likely to be a topic customers are actually talking about.

Instead, you should be looking for topics that people are already talking about that also allow you to introduce your product or new idea.

Remember the example of the company that wanted to introduce a new platform for sales forecasting? Talking about their new product was exciting, and they were able to rank on Page One for their newly minted product terms with no problem. Unfortunately, no one was actually searching for those terms because no one knew they existed. People were searching for information on how to use Excel, and their competitors owned the traffic around Excel. When the company changed their tactic and met customers where they were, they were able to make a case for their new solution.

As you gather and compare your rankings and your competitors' rankings on the smaller cluster of topics left on your list, consider your customers' pain rather than your specific solution. Where do you rank on the topics that reflect what customers actually care about? Even if the question or topic doesn't have anything to do with your product specifically, it can be the most valuable one to own if it solves a customer's pain most directly.

If a key competitor is ranking high for a keyword or question related specifically to the customer pain you'd like to solve, going all in to own that topic might be the best starting point for your content. Or alternately, if there is a keyword or question your competitors aren't ranking for at all, choosing it might give you a quick win, especially if it's closely related to your niche in the market.

By the end of the prioritization process, you will have a three-dimensional map of the entire network of terms and questions related to your proposed topics. The map provides a complete list of possible topics, how they are related, and the central hubs through which the majority of customers are traveling on their buying journeys. You will have a comparison of search volumes for the highest-value terms across the network. And you will have a clear view of where you currently rank for the terms you care about—and where your competitors rank as well.

Together, these insights enable you to transition from the old, guesswork-based, "see what sticks" method to an informed, educated, data-grounded strategy of laser-focused efficiency. You will be able to choose one Pillar Topic to start with, knowing with certainty that it is your highest-value target.

PBM IN PRACTICE

Let's see where Jennifer is in her process. When she started comparing her topics, she already knew that the majority of EasySigner's customers were interested in electronic signatures, so it seemed obvious to choose this as her first Pillar Topic. But when she visualized the network and compared the topics to each other, she saw something different:

	Topic	Est Monthly Searches	Total Discovered Keywords	Ranking Keywords (You)	Ranking Keywords (Competitors)
1	document generation	98,445,230	1,997	416	477
2	document generation for financial services	85,300,520	716	203	180
3	electronic signature for financial services	39,725,280	1,015	751	663
4	document generation for insurance	5,701,430	563	29	40
5	electronic signature	1,851,720	90	78	82
6	digital document management	46,130	81	6	20
7	electronic signature for insurance	10	0	0	0

Within a single dashboard in DemandJump, Jennifer can compare the net search volume not just for one keyword but for the entire spiderweb of relevant keywords and questions for each of her potential Pillar Topics. She can quickly compare the size of each network, including where she and her competitors currently rank for terms in those networks, and she can even click into the title of each potential Pillar Topic to take a direct look at the specific terms contained in each spiderweb to ensure her chosen Pillar Topic has plenty of keywords that relate directly to her market and her solution.

By generating and visualizing the three-dimensional spiderweb of search terms and comparing total monthly search volumes across the entire network, Jennifer sees that "document generation" has far more potential overall: higher total search volumes, more relevance to her business goals, and more potential to make gains over competitors. Additionally, when Jennifer reviews the spiderwebs around her industry-specific Pillar Topic options, she finds a jumbled mess of terms specific to electronic signatures and terms about finance or insurance—not terms about electronic signature applications for those industries, which is what she cares about. Using the DemandJump platform, she was able to see all this information in minutes, not months.

STEP THREE: PLANT YOUR FLAG

Here you are, at the moment of decision. With all the information you've gained from the prioritization process, you will know—better than you ever could have known before—which of your potential Pillar Topics has the right balance of search volume, importance in the overall network of related terms and questions, relevance to the pain you're trying to solve, and potential for improving your rankings compared to competitors. When you find this balance, you know that you have a good topic.

Some companies get to this point and start to get cold feet. They are so used to trying to own every keyword, to not lose a single customer, that they are afraid to commit to a single topic. They ask us, "Why do I need just one Pillar Topic to start with? Can't I increase my impact by having more?"

The answer to that is, yes. You could potentially increase your impact by taking on multiple high-value topics right away.

If you had the resources.

But here's the rub: we have found again and again that producing a significant volume of content around a given Pillar Topic is critical to gaining rankings over competitors who are trying to do the same thing. We'll talk in more detail about the specifics later, but we generally recommend that an initial content launch for any Pillar should contain at least 16 pieces of content (one Pillar Page, three Sub-Pillar Pages, three Supporting Blogs corresponding to each Sub-Pillar Page, and three for the Pillar Page) and that these should be launched as quickly as possible—with all the content going live over the course of just a few days, or sometimes less.

Because the goal is to publish a whole network made up of the right content all at once, we have found that the best strategy for almost any brand is to tackle one topic at a time. Focusing all your content creation resources on a single topic allows you to gain exponentially faster ranking results than any other approach. So unless you know you have the resources to go hard and fast on more than one topic right away, starting with one Pillar Topic is the best way to deploy your investment while maximizing the potential impact of your new content.

In other words: plant your flag. Choose that one powerful, high-value Pillar Topic based on all the information you've gathered, and commit to it. The Pillar Topic you choose will be the clear winner when you compare it to the others in a dashboard like the one we shared just a few pages ago, where you can easily compare everything from search volume to the size of the prize to your current competitive rankings.

This is where you will start to see how widely Pillar-Based Marketing differs from your previous approaches, because you won't have to wait long or live with anxiety while you wait to see results. If you commit to one Pillar Topic and then follow the strategy we lay out in the next few chapters, you will see results more quickly than you could have imagined—within a few weeks, not six months or longer. Once you see those results for your first topic, you will definitely want to add new content or new Pillar Topics, and we'll show you how to do that, too.

THE TAKEAWAY

Before we talk about how to implement your new Pillar Topic, let's check in with Jennifer one more time. What has changed for her as she has worked through this process?

The best part for Jennifer is that she has definitively selected "document generation" as her first Pillar Topic. She can now design a strategy around that topic without worrying about whether she should have chosen "electronic signature" or some other related topic. She also knows that producing content around document generation topics, rather than around Easy-Signer's specific product features, will net her an exponentially larger network and exponentially more of the network's traffic of existing searches.

She can present clear data to prove which direction the company should put its content marketing resources into. She has confidence that the decision she's proposing is a good one—and maybe even more importantly, an *objective* one. She can skip the brainstorming meetings and the arguments about whose instincts are right, removing a whole time-consuming and wasteful step in the process and going straight to a decision in a fraction of the time. She has a clear, data-driven direction that she can commit to and convince others to commit to.

Perhaps best of all, she won't find herself writing dozens of pieces of content that end up going nowhere. There will be none of the wasted time and effort and energy and anxiety that went with her previous strategies.

Similarly, if you go through the process outlined here, the discovery you've undertaken in Step One will lead you to a targeted, single Pillar to focus your strategy around. You'll be able to see the "size of the prize"—how much traffic is available for each potential pillar—and select with confidence the one that will get your company the greatest impact, the most traffic, and the Page One rankings you need to drive revenue.

In the next chapter, we'll show you how to create your Pillar Strategy, using your content to mirror the search network and become the world's expert on your chosen Pillar Topic.

CHAPTER 8

BUILDING YOUR PILLAR STRATEGY

Congratulations! You've chosen your first Pillar Topic. That's a big win: you now have the confidence to build a strategy around your topic, knowing that it's the one with the greatest potential to gain the rankings you want on the topics of interest to your customers. Well done!

But while choosing a first Pillar Topic feels like a victory—and it is—there is still the potential for a lot of wasted time, effort, and resources if you don't know what to *do* with it. Even though you've chosen a Pillar Topic and committed to it, there are still literally millions of different ways you could write about it. You still have questions to address, many of them previously impossible to answer objectively. How many pieces should you create? What exact topics should you write about? What length should they be? How should they be related to each other?

Your Pillar Topic is the main interstate, the term at the center of the search network. It's where people who are interested in your topic end up, even if many of them don't start there. All roads, so to speak, lead to the Pillar Topic.

Now it's time to build those roads.

If someone in your life asked you how to get to your house, you wouldn't start your instructions with, "I have a blue front door and a big sunflower garden." Those might be true statements about your house, and they might be things your friend will ultimately be interested in. But they won't matter—they won't help your friend find you—until she is already driving down your block.

Traditional approaches to content strategy are like telling your friend about your front door one week, then waiting and telling them about your sunflowers the next week, and maybe a week after that, talking about what neighborhood you're in. Not only is all the content about your house (rather than being about where the friend is right now), but it's spread out over such a long time period that she's probably forgotten your last instruction by the time she gets the next one.

Okay, okay—it's a long analogy. But it points out the critical differences between the typical "editorial calendar" approach to content strategy and the PBM strategy.

The most common way for marketers to design their strategy is to select a set of four or five (or sometimes six or eight or even more) topics or types of content, then schedule their team to write and publish on those various topics once or twice or even ten times a week, generally cycling through the topics or types of content over the course of each month.

Jennifer's company, EasySigner, for example, has been publishing two pieces of content a week. Based on their best guesses and the data they have available, they cycle through pieces on their product's main features, case studies, and user-generated questions. This piecemeal approach can add up to a lot of information about your product, but it won't make search engines see your company as an authority on any single topic that customers care about, and it won't give customers a path from where they are to where you want them to be.

Your Pillar Strategy turns this traditional approach on its head. A Pillar Strategy is not about covering every topic or piecing out information about your company over time. It's about building an entire map—a network of interrelated content that will lead your customers by the hand through topics they are interested in, right to your door—and giving it to them all at once.

In more concrete terms, building your Pillar Strategy means translating the network around your Pillar Topic into a set of multiple hierarchical pieces of content, with the main page about your Pillar Topic at the top of the hierarchy and more specific, longer-tail content connected to it. The Pillar Topic content on your site becomes a miniature version of the real-world network of questions and topics that customers are searching, essentially recreating their search journey on your site.

If choosing a first Pillar Topic is about figuring out the exact topic to commit to out of all the many variations of that topic, building your strategy is about determining exactly which pieces of content to write, out of all the millions of potential combinations. And just like choosing a topic, this step is data-driven and aligned with real customer behavior.

In this chapter, you will learn not only which pieces of content to produce first but how many to write, how long they should be, how they should relate to each other, and how all the pieces will work together to drive engagement and Page One rankings across the entire network all at once.

As we have helped hundreds of customers develop, publish, and refine content, we have been able to experiment and gather data and refine the Pillar Strategy for content within the framework of PBM. The result is a highly sophisticated, data-driven, and precise methodology for choosing the initial subtopics to write about, how long to make each of the pieces, and how to link and publish the content to get the fastest, most powerful ranking results. We'll discuss writing and publishing in the next two chapters; this chapter will show you how to plan what content you will write by selecting your initial Sub-Pillar and Supporting Blog topics.

Let's do it.

THE FUNDAMENTALS

At the most basic level, your Pillar Strategy is about becoming part of the conversation your potential customers are already engaged in by building a smaller version of the Pillar Topic network on your own domain.

Your customers are already out on the internet, engaging in search behavior, seeking answers to their questions and information about the topics they are interested in. That behavior generates the network of topics and keywords we discussed in the previous chapter. The purpose of your Pillar Strategy is to recreate a portion of that network with a set of related content pieces that all work together to mirror the ways that real people are searching for your Pillar Topic online.

The network is the real world—the way people are already engaging with the Pillar Topic online—and the content you choose to create determines how you engage with that network. You choose which on-ramps to be present at, in other words. And as with everything else in PBM, this process is data-driven and objective. To build your strategy, you identify all the subtopics and long-tail questions that most commonly drive organic traffic toward the Pillar Topic you are interested in, and you write content to address those subtopics and questions, all leading toward and connecting to your main Pillar Topic.

Your Pillar Strategy, in other words, unwinds the three-dimensional, complexly interconnected network into a linear, top-down hierarchy of content that makes your site a mirror of customers' real-world search behavior.

Remember this graphic from Section 1? We promised we'd come back to how the DemandJump platform unwinds the spiderweb around a given Pillar Topic, so here's another look at what happens when you translate our earlier example of the "hurricane season" Pillar Topic into a hierarchical Pillar Strategy.

THE CONTENT PYRAMID

While your traditional content strategy may have involved generating a calendar of weekly or biweekly blog posts, your Pillar Strategy will instead provide a map of related pieces of content that are connected in a very specific way. To start, you will write one long-form Pillar Page, supported by three slightly shorter Sub-Pillar Pages, each of which is in turn supported by three Supporting Blogs on niche long-tail topics. Overall, the strategy resembles a pyramid, a hierarchy of content flowing up to and supporting the Pillar Page.

In its basic form, your Pillar Strategy looks like this:

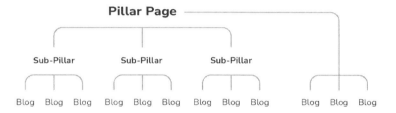

The **Pillar Page** (one long-form piece of content) shares its name with your Pillar Topic and addresses the highest-level, broadest content. It's both the hub of your content network and the top of your content pyramid.

Sub-Pillar Pages (three slightly shorter pieces of content) can be either main navigation pages or blog posts, and they address topics that are more specific than your Pillar Topic but directly related to it, covering various aspects of your Pillar Topic in more detail. For example, if Jennifer at EasySigner has chosen "document generation" as her Pillar Topic, her Sub-Pillar pages might include "document generation software," "document generation types," or "document generation examples." She will choose these subtopics based on the data from the network in a process we will explain later in the chapter.

Supporting Blogs (twelve short-form pieces of content), the bottom of the pyramid, share their titles with high-value long-tail keywords and commonly asked questions. They provide more detail and generally offer immediate, practical value related to a specific customer need or pain point. For example, Jennifer at EasySign might choose "What is an example of automated document generation?" as one of her Supporting Blog questions—which would connect up to the Sub-Pillar Topic of "document generation examples."

You will write three Supporting Blogs for each of your Sub-Pillar Pages and three for your main Pillar Page: twelve Supporting Blogs in all.

Again, we'll talk more about selecting your specific blog topics below. We'll also address how best to use keywords, and how many keywords to use in each piece, in Chapter 9.

> Together, the Pillar Page, Sub-Pillar Pages, and Supporting Blogs make up the 16 pieces of your initial Pillar Strategy.

You might remember from Chapter 6 that when we wanted to rank on Page One for the keyword "content marketing," we developed 89 pieces and posted them all at once. We decided that was necessary for such a highly competitive keyword in a field already dominated by other content marketers—and it was also an initial test of the PBM approach. Since then, through our work with hundreds of companies, we have seen again and again that 16 pieces is enough to start ranking on almost any topic a customer wants to own.

There are several reasons why 16 is a kind of magic number. Having 16 pieces of content allows you to build out several supporting Sub-Pillars that link up to the main Pillar Page without being too overwhelming or resource-heavy. Our data shows that 16 pieces is enough to create your mini-spiderweb and convince search engines that you are a real authority on the Pillar Topic—that you're not just writing a one-off SEO article. It's enough to rank without overburdening your writers.

As you'll see in Chapter 11, there will be times when you want to develop more content, or add to your existing pieces, after you start to see how they are performing. But as an initial strategy, 16 is the sweet spot to create the network effect we're working for and start ranking on Page One for whatever Pillar Topic you've chosen.

ELEMENTS OF THE PILLAR STRATEGY

One interesting thing about a truly data-driven strategy is that it can provide insights into every part of your process, even details like the best length for each piece of content you create.

In the past, there have been a lot of assumptions around the best length for content. Many marketers still believe that customers simply won't read long pieces, with many claiming that no piece of content should be longer than a couple of hundred words. Others look at the average length of time spent on their website and write content to fit that amount of reading time. Many blogs even post an estimated reading time for each piece, on the assumption that readers are in a hurry and don't want to engage with long content.

Nothing could be further from the truth.

The truth about content length is this: readers will engage with long content if it answers the questions they are asking and addresses the real need they have in searching for the content in the first place. What they will click away from quickly is content that is poorly written, doesn't align with their needs, or attempts to sell to them prematurely.

After all, the people who are searching for content are seeking out information. They *want* information—as much as they can get—as long as it is about their needs, not yours. We have seen pieces of content run into thousands of words and engage readers all the way to the end. In fact, it's downright common for practitioners of PBM to see average time on page for Pillar Pages of 3,000 or more words reach ten minutes or more. (More on that in Chapter 11.) The right length of each piece depends on the type of content, where in their journey the customer encounters it, and the question or topic it's addressing.

Our work has allowed us to experiment with content length, and the result is a very clear picture of the most successful length for each piece of your content strategy.

- In general, your Pillar Page—the main "hub" for your strategy that addresses the Pillar Topic directly—should be 3,000 words or more. Yes, you read that correctly. More than 3,000 words. If you have chosen your Pillar Topic based on network data as we outlined in Chapter 7, this will be the central topic, the most common point of interest, for your target audience, and they will be happy to get as much information as you can provide. (In Chapter 9, we will show you exactly how to design and write that content to keep them engaged.)

- **Your Sub-Pillar Pages, on the three supporting subtopics that link up to your Pillar Page, should be around 2,000 words.** We talk below about how to select and prioritize your Sub-Pillar Topics; for now, it's sufficient to understand that these should be slightly more specific topics and keywords that are directly linked to your Pillar Topic in the spiderweb. They address topics and questions that searchers often engage with on their way to your main Pillar Topic, and they will play the same function in your Pillar Strategy, moving readers toward your Pillar Page.

- **Finally, your Supporting Blogs should be about 700 words,** sometimes a bit more. Supporting Blogs address niche or long-tail topics or questions, which are often the first places searchers start out before they end up at your Pillar Topic. Think of these as the side streets or "feeder" roads, which lead customers to the main roads (your Sub-Pillar Pages), which take them directly to the main highway outside your front door (your Pillar Page). Supporting Blogs address specific questions that commonly show up in the spiderweb as connected to your Pillar Topic. They are often the first entry points for your customers to engage with your content.

Altogether, these 16 pieces of content represent a fully fleshed-out portion of the real-world search network. They provide the opportunity for potential customers to engage with you at any point in their search journey (research, evaluation, and decision), whether they are in the initial stages of searching very narrow questions related to their immediate pain points or actively looking for new solutions. And most importantly, because the topic and content of each piece is based on the real-world search data, the finished mini-network is highly aligned to customer behavior.

Keep in mind that these length suggestions come as the result of trial and error across thousands of published pieces of PBM content. If your Pillar Page can accomplish its goal of answering the broadest questions people have about your Pillar Topic in just 2,600 words, that can work—as long as your Pillar Page does a better job of addressing the topic than the other pieces of content that are already ranking on Page One. In other words, the length of content generally comes down to providing the best user experience, even if that means bending the rules laid out here.

When you publish this collection of 16 pieces of content, you will have recreated right on your own website the portion of the entire internet that is most highly relevant to your Pillar Topic. That's when search engines start to see you as the world authority on that topic—and rank your content high as a result, not because you are gaming the system, but because you provide content readers want. After all, that's what search engines are designed to do.

PBM IN ACTION

Building your Pillar Strategy is essentially like choosing your first Pillar Topic in miniature. In fact, each step of the PBM process, from choosing your first Pillar Topic, to selecting which Sub-Pillars to write about, to determining exactly what to include in each piece of content, requires the same basic steps of understanding the network of real search behavior and prioritizing the most important, common, or central topics and questions.

In other words, at each step in the PBM process, you will dig deeper into the spiderweb. When you choose your first Pillar Topic, you look at the entire network for all the potential keywords you are interested in. To set your Pillar Strategy, you zoom into the network for just that one topic, seeking out the subtopics, specific questions, and long-tail keywords related to it. Then you prioritize which of those you will write about, based again on how central, how interconnected, and how common each of the potential subtopics is.

There are three main steps to building your Pillar Strategy: generating the list of potential Sub-Pillar Topics, prioritizing that list, and then building an aggregate network around your selections.

GENERATE YOUR LIST

The first step in building your Pillar Strategy is to generate a list of subtopics and long-tail questions and keywords related, in the real-world search network, to your Pillar Topic. Just like with choosing your Pillar Topic, you could build your list through painstaking manual searching, although it would take an inordinate amount of time—and would not show you the connections and relationships among the topics.

Using the DemandJump platform, however, automatically provides a networked list with specific recommendations for individual blog posts grouped under the Sub-Pillars they fall under.

Remember Jennifer at EasySigner? Here is a partial example of what the list looks like for her Pillar Topic, "document generation."

	Pillar Page	Sub-Pillar Page	Supporting Blog
1	document generation	free document editing software for windows 10	What program can I use to edit documents for free?
2	document generation	free document editing software for windows 10	What is the best free document editor?
3	document generation	free document editing software for windows 10	Is there a free word processing program for Windows 10?
4	document generation	free document editing software for windows 10	Is there a free PDF editor for Windows 10?
5	document generation	best document creation software	Which software is used for document creation?
6	document generation	best document creation software	Which software helps us to create documents easily?
7	document generation	best document creation software	What is the best program to create documents?
8	document generation	best document creation software	What is the best free document editor?
9	document generation	free document generation software	What is the best program to create documents?
10	document generation	free document generation software	Is Docassemble free?
11	document generation	free document generation software	How do I create a free document?
12	document generation	free document generation software	How do I automate a document for free?
13	document generation	conga support	What does conga software do?
14	document generation	conga support	Is Conga part of Salesforce?
15	document generation	conga support	Is Apttus now conga?
16	document generation	conga support	How do I contact conga support?»
17	document generation	document generator free	Where can I create a document for free?
18	document generation	document generator free	What is the best program to create documents?
19	document generation	document generator free	What is a document generator?
20	document generation	document generator free	How can I create my own document?
21	document generation	document generation salesforce	What is Salesforce document generation?
22	document generation	document generation salesforce	What is conga document generation?
23	document generation	document generation salesforce	What is a document generation tool?
24	document generation	document generation salesforce	Can Salesforce create documents?

In the DemandJump dashboard designed to automate your Pillar Strategy, you'll see keywords and questions from your Pillar Topic's spiderweb automatically designated as the titles of Pillar Pages, Sub-Pillar Pages, and Supporting Blogs based on their contextual relevance, length, and importance to the broader structure of the network.

Notice that you can see a comprehensive list of recommended blog post ideas, based on real-world searches and sorted by subtopics. Each of these is a potential Sub-Pillar Page. One level down, you will see that each subtopic is broken down further, into specific questions that are the titles of proposed Supporting Blogs. Each specific question has been identified, by the machine-learning process, as being directly linked to the subtopic it is grouped under. In other words, search data shows that people who search that specific question also searched for the more general subtopic term or keyword. Related questions all link up to a Sub-Pillar Topic with which they have an affinity in the data, and all the Sub-Pillar Topics are the terms that have an affinity with your Pillar Topic.

The key here is that the more times a particular question or key-word phrase shows up, the more common it is in the real-world search data. In many cases, a particular question will show up under multiple subtopics, suggesting that many people who end up at your Pillar Topic search that question, no matter the path they took or where they started their search. Identifying which three Sub-Pillar Topics, and which four Supporting Blog questions, to address in your initial Pillar Strategy is the key to building your content network.

If you are using the DemandJump platform, please note you will see things that are branded with your competitors' names and sometimes things that seemingly don't make any sense.

This is because what you are seeing is the real search behavior that search engines see and not what users see. You won't necessarily write about your competitors, and sometimes you will see things that are not part of what you actually sell.

The breakthrough, though, is seeing any given Pillar Topic's real-world network and then choosing how you desire to be a part of that network by writing about the most important, powerful, and connected customer behavior that will drive the target market to you.

Remember when we talked about a sales forecasting SaaS company deciding to write about Microsoft Excel? They made that decision based on the data from their chosen Pillar Topic spiderweb. We should note here, however, that the SaaS company involved was committed to publishing many dozens of pieces of content. If they were starting with just 16 pieces, using branded keywords belonging to their competition would have taken a lower priority.

The point is this: the data represents the real world. Making your final choice of topics to write about requires every bit of creativity and human thinking that the rest of marketing does. Speaking of which...

PRIORITIZE YOUR LIST

Once you have generated the list of all the subtopics and specific questions related to your Pillar Topic, you have to decide which ones to choose for your initial 16 pieces of content.

When you use the DemandJump platform, the technology places a priority on each term for you, a score that shows you exactly how important that term or question is to the overall network. The priority score is assigned based on a number of factors, including the search volume for the specific question or term, how frequently it appears across different parts of the network, and how many other keyword phrases branch off of it. Together, all of this data shows you how frequently people interact with this individual term or question as they go through their buying process—no matter where in the network they enter or what path they follow.

Taking all that information together, the platform assigns a score that indicates how critical that particular Sub-Pillar term is to the overall network, including its connectivity to other key terms and how close it is to the central hub.

Essentially, this is the same process content marketers have always used when they've had to decide what to write about—trying to determine which topics and subtopics will be of greatest interest to their customers. But in the past, choosing the specific content to write has been frightening and hard because there has been no way to know whether you are writing about the most important topics or leaving out something critical.

Instead of paving a square foot here and a side road there and a cul-de-sac off by itself, network data shows you how to build roads where your customers already are.

> Our technology shows that there can be thousands of phrases, questions, and subtopics related to a single Pillar Topic—so the fear that you could be missing something is well founded. That's why we built the DemandJump platform, to analyze multiple points of data for each term or question across the entire network and determine which are the most important. We've said it before, and we'll say it again: as far as we know, the DemandJump platform is the only technology that provides this kind of insight.

Just like you chose one Pillar Topic to start with, you will use your network data to select the three highest-priority Sub-Pillar Topics, and the four most important Supporting Blog questions for each, and focus on creating world-class content for each one. There is always more you can do, but building your Pillar Strategy is about seeing, and confidently concentrating your efforts and resources on, the most important parts of the network.

After reviewing all of the recommendations for potential articles in her "document generation" Pillar Strategy, Jennifer followed these steps to identify the three Sub-Pillar Topics that were of the highest priority and most aligned with both EasySigner and their customers. She chose three of the recommended Supporting Blogs under each of those Sub-Pillar Topics. She then reviewed all of the recommended Supporting Blogs to choose another three to produce and link directly to her Pillar Page on document generation.

Here's a look at Jenifer's finished 16-piece Pillar Strategy:

This Pillar Strategy tool is available on DemandJump University to help you organize your chosen articles and manage them through the writing and publishing process.

BUILD AN AGGREGATE NETWORK

Finally, as you develop your Pillar Strategy, remember that this process is not about single terms or individual blog posts. One blog post or keyword by itself might not—in fact, almost certainly won't—get you the leads you want, but the *aggregate* of your entire network will.

One of the most powerful parts of the PBM approach is the way each element of the network supports all the others. Because your content is interconnected, when one post performs better, they all perform better. Very often, when customers write their first Pillar Topic content, they see other content on their website—even content that may have been written years ago and isn't related to the Pillar Page at all—suddenly get increased traffic as well.

That happens because search engines will start to see your site as a central hub for the entire topic. Your aggregate network of content shows them that you understand the entire topic, that you are a thought leader, and not just using SEO to game the system.

The same is true for ranking: it's about the aggregate effect of all your content. We see over and over that customers can rank higher when they write all the content around a topic—owning all the niche questions and key subtopics—than with content only on the main topic itself.

You can watch a detailed walk-through of the Pillar Strategy decision-making process at DemandJump University, at DemandJump.com. While you're there, you can also get fully certified in Pillar-Based Marketing strategy by completing each of the PBM steps!

THE TAKEAWAY

At the end of this step, you will know the specific pieces of content you are going to write to drive traffic and leads and customers. You won't have to wonder what to write about or which of the literally thousands of possible subtopics and niche questions to address because you will know the specific central, and critical, topics relevant to the network of real search behavior. You will have a plan for 16 pieces of content that will recreate that network on your own website, with a detailed understanding of how long each piece should be and how all the elements of the content hierarchy work together to support your overall Pillar Topic.

Best of all, you will have objective data to back up your choices. That is what confidence feels like.

So now, with your Pillar Strategy in hand, all you have to do is decide what to actually write. That's the focus of your next step.

CHAPTER 9

CREATING YOUR PILLAR CONTENT

Finally, it's time to write.

You've chosen a Pillar Topic and decided which 16 pieces of content to start with. You know what your content pyramid looks like and how your Sub-Pillar pieces and your Supporting Blogs support your Pillar Page. You have presented your data-driven strategy to your CEO, CMO, VP of marketing, manager, or client and gotten the go-ahead to implement it.

Excellent! Now what?

Now it's time to sit down with your writers and give them their assignments. But you find yourself yet again in the same position: although you know what topics to write about, there are a million ways your writers could create the content itself. How should you use the Pillar Topic terms, if at all, in each piece you write? How should you include keywords? How should you answer the questions customers are asking—and how do you know exactly what information they are seeking when they ask those questions?

You're moving from high-level strategy into the details of the content creation process, deciding on specific words, phrases, headers, and blog titles. How can you best prepare your writers to maximize the value of the content strategy you've devised?

It's simple: you apply the same network logic to each individual piece of content. Take the same spiderweb approach that you applied to the entire network of search behavior to choose your Pillar Topic, and to your Pillar Topic to determine your Sub-Pillar Topics. You will do the same analysis, only on the micro level, performing the same exercise you did for your whole topic, but for this one piece. The result is a mini-network of branching keywords and questions that reflect the information customers are trying to learn when they engage with a specific subtopic or question.

Each piece of content you write will reflect its own mini-universe of connected subtopics and niche concerns, using keywords, questions, and headers in a proven way that keeps readers engaged and ranks well with search engines.

But first, try to forget everything you think you know about SEO and using keywords in your content.

THE FUNDAMENTALS

The first step to creating great Pillar Content that maximizes the impact—and the overall network effect—of your Pillar Strategy is to forget everything you thought you knew about how to use keywords in your content. We have learned what is important and not important about keyword usage, and we're going to show you the best practices we've developed over hundreds and hundreds of iterations.

The key to writing engaging content that also informs search engines that you are an authority on your topic is understanding and using the whole network of keywords around a subtopic or niche question, rather than focusing on just one or two.

FORGET WHAT YOU THINK YOU KNOW

There are a lot of myths and assumptions out there about how to use keywords in writing organic content. We want to spend most of this chapter talking about what you *should* do to get the results you want, but we need to address these elephants in the room first.

- **Myth #1: You need to use your keyword or keywords multiple times in an article.** A very popular myth, this belief is based on the idea that search engines give higher rankings to articles that use the same keywords over and over, as if they see the article as more likely to be "about" that topic, or relevant to it, if it uses the topic term more than once. There used to be some truth to this belief, but search engines have intentionally set out to change their practices in response to overuse. If you use a keyword in your article once, you're done. Using keywords multiple times in each piece can be hard to give up if you've always done it, but the benefits go beyond improved rankings: your content will also come across to readers as more natural and authentic. That's a win-win.

- **Myth #2: You need to maximize keyword density.** This myth is similar to the first one. Some content graders will tell you that each keyword needs to make up a certain percentage of an article (have a certain "keyword density") in order to be competitive in search engine results. Again, this isn't true anymore, if it ever was. Rather than focusing on using certain words a particular number of times or making some specific percentage of the article those words, you need to provide keywords that indicate the *exact* aspect or element of the topic you're covering.
- **Myth #3: You should never use the same keyword in two pieces of content.** We'll talk more about this later, but for now just know this: it doesn't really matter. Many marketers are afraid that their content will "compete with itself" for search rankings if more than one article uses the same keyword. But if you are using the network approach, you are already building each piece of content to support each other piece, and the network as a whole. If you choose keywords and topic phrases that target each piece of content to the specific aspect of the topic it is intended to cover, the pieces will not compete with but complement each other—especially if you follow the interlinking strategy we lay out here to strengthen the flow of information within your content network.

These myths continue to be popular in part because many marketers use content graders, such as the WordPress Yoast SEO plug-in and others, to assign an SEO score to their content before posting it. The belief is that a high score on a content grader will lead to better rankings. But most of these tools are built on outdated legacy SEO rules—specifically, the myths listed above.

While it is easy to grade a piece of content based on how many times a specific word shows up, and while it can be reassuring to get a high score before posting your content, these graders don't reflect the fast-changing realities of modern search engine algorithms.

How do we know this? Because we've driven the remarkable results we've described in this book thus far for hundreds of PBM practitioners without ever considering a single one of these vestigial "best practices." They just don't matter in the face of the network-driven approach to content we're empowering you to implement.

So if the old rules don't apply, how can you know exactly what to write?

THE NEXT LEVEL DOWN IN THE NETWORK

At each step in the PBM process, your goal is to visualize, prioritize, and apply the network of interconnected terms and questions around a topic, starting at the macro level when choosing your Pillar Topic and narrowing down to identify Sub-Pillar and Supporting Blog topics as you develop your strategy.

In the content-writing stage, you go through the same process again in miniature, identifying the network of specific questions and keywords related to each of your Sub-Pillar and

Supporting Blog titles. For example, if Jennifer at EasySigner has decided to create a Sub-Pillar page titled "free document generation software," she would start developing her content by analyzing the real-world search data around that specific term. Whereas before, when she was determining her Pillar Strategy, she viewed the entire search network around the broad term of "document generation," she is now looking more deeply, and more narrowly, at just that portion of the network related to the title of this specific Sub-Pillar Page.

As with the earlier steps, she will start to see patterns of hubs and spokes, with questions and terms that people search very often showing up many times, and questions and terms that are common to multiple search pathways appearing as hubs. Once she has this network in hand, she will be able to determine the most important concerns to cover, and questions to answer, in her Sub-Pillar Page content.

Free Document Generation Software
Keywords to Include:
- Free document editing apps for Android
- Free document editing software for Windows 10
- Best document editing software
- Best free document editing software
- Document editing software free download
- Free document generation software
- Free document automation software
- Document generation software

Related Questions to Include/Answer:

- Is there a free document editor?
- What is the best free document editor?
- Is Docassemble free?
- What is the best document editing software?
- Is there a free Word program for Windows 10?
- What is automatic document generation?
- Free document generation software
- What is Salesforce document generation?
- What is a document generation?
- What is automated document generation?

This example list based on Jennifer's EasySigner needs represents just a small selection of the keyword and question recommendations the DemandJump platform can provide for any article you'd like to write.

Having the list in hand, though, is not enough by itself. As you decide what to write, you also need to know how many of the keywords to choose, which ones to focus on, and how to structure your content around them.

PBM IN ACTION

We've talked about this before, but we're going to mention it again: we love data. Data can give us certainty where there was only guesswork and instinct. It can provide comfort and confidence where before we had anxiety and even fear. And that's not just true across the big picture; data can provide insights on the nitty-gritty decisions, like what words to choose and how to arrange them on the page. That still seems pretty exciting to us.

But marketers have struggled to make sense of the data they have to inform the actions to take next. This is the entire foundation of Pillar-Based Marketing: making sense of the data so you can be confident that the decisions you make will drive your desired go-to-market strategy and achieve your company's goals. Not to mention that you sleep better at night.

Based on our years of data and experimentation, we have derived four best practices for keyword usage that should drive the creation of your content:

- Pick the right number of keywords.
- Choose questions first.
- Use those questions in second-level headings.
- Include Pillar and Sub-Pillar Topic titles in your content.

We'll talk about each of these in detail below.

PICK THE RIGHT NUMBER OF KEYWORDS

The traditional approach to keywords has been to choose one or two for each article and then sprinkle them liberally and repeatedly throughout the text. But as we pointed out above, not only is that tedious (and generally unhelpful) for readers, it also doesn't work for modern search engines. Modern search engines use sophisticated algorithms to determine whether your content is (a) what searches are looking for and (b) a source of authentic expertise on a topic. That also means that the approach of cramming as many keywords as possible into one long article isn't going to work because it ignores the user's needs in a similar way.

Choosing and using the right keywords—*all* the right keywords—in your article is how you do that.

Choosing the right keywords starts with seeing the entire network of related terms and questions. Once you have your list, the next step is knowing how many to choose. This is one of those areas that seems like it should be subjective, or variable. The data says otherwise. Across the thousands of articles we've written to help customers get to Page One, we have found that certain numbers of keywords establish authority and relevance for search engines for different lengths of articles.

In general, here are those best practices:

- Pillar Pages, which are 3,000+ words, should include about 20 keywords.
- Sub-Pillar Pages, at 2,000 words or so, should include 15 keywords.
- Supporting Blogs, at 750 words, give or take, should include 7–8 keywords.

This level of specificity, and the sheer number of keywords included in the longer articles, shocks some marketers. The numbers bear it out, though. Again and again we've found that these numbers of keywords strike just the right balance between maximizing the organic reach of each article (since each article covers multiple searchable keywords) and structuring each article to meet readers' expectations (since we can cover each keyword in enough detail to provide value to the reader).

Remember, modern search engines care more about how engaging a piece of content is, based on how long readers spend on the page and how much they interact with it, than they do about how often a specific word shows up. So maximizing the number of customers who come to the page and how aligned it is with their expectations and needs is the best way to move up in the rankings.

We all know the statistics about how long readers typically spend on any given web page. They are dismal. According to HubSpot, the longest average time spent on a web page is one minute and 37 seconds, which is in B2B. Other sectors such as energy and grocery average an appalling 44 seconds. In contrast, marketers leveraging Pillar-Based Marketing see times averaging anywhere between 5 and 15 minutes. Why? Because the content is truly aligned to the pain or problem the user is trying to solve or the desire they are seeking to fulfill.

The PBM perspective is to see the keywords you choose to target in a given piece of content not as a list of valuable targets in and of themselves but as a set of instructions for your writers that details exactly what to cover in each piece of content. The happy accident that results is that across 16 pieces of Pillar Content, you may find yourself increasing your rankings for 130 or more keywords.

More important than any quantitative metric around the number of keywords you target, however, is the function this number of keywords serves. It's not just about casting the widest possible net and hoping to "win" on as many keywords as possible. It's about understanding *exactly* what people are searching for around the topics you're choosing to write about. When you structure your Pillar Content around relevant and important keywords related to each topic, you are informing your writing process to focus only on what your reader cares about.

That's how the network effect of PBM begins to drive outsized organic traffic in such a short time; you're using data to inform every decision, from which pieces to write, to the creative direction of those pieces. In other words, you're prioritizing the needs of real people asking real questions, and you're rewarded as an authority with Page One rankings as a result.

CHOOSE QUESTIONS FIRST

Truly engaging and customer-aligned content starts with addressing and answering the questions customers are asking. Focusing your content around those questions provides a structure for your articles, gives you specific ideas to write about, and helps readers see that your content is valuable to them.

When you are looking at the mini-network of keywords and topics related to each Sub-Pillar Topic or Supporting Blog title to better understand the topics to write about in each piece, you should search for and include questions first. Questions are the most common way people search for information, and they tend to be longer-tail, more specific reflections of the information people are actually trying to find. If you write your content to address those questions directly, you will be directly aligned with customer behavior and needs.

Plus, if you know that your job as a writer is to answer a specific set of questions, you no longer have to wonder what to write. You just have to gather information and provide context and insight around those particular answers.

PBM IN PRACTICE

As an example, here are some questions related to the topic of "document generation" that Jennifer might choose as keywords for EasySigner's Pillar Page:

Related questions to include/answer:

- Can documentation be automated?
- Which software is used for creating documents?
- What software is used to make documents?
- What is document preparation software?
- What is a document generator?
- Which is the best software to create general documents?
- What does it mean to automate a document?
- What is the best program to create documents?

The Content Brief tool in DemandJump provides the same sort of "contextual" analysis of related queries for each piece of content you write as it does for your broader Pillar Topic.

Your job is not just to dump keywords into your article, even if the keywords are the exact questions customers are asking. Although this could attract attention to your page initially, it's not going to drive real engagement or rankings. Your job is to provide world-class, authentic, high-quality answers to those questions. So once you use your network data to determine which search questions are most closely related to the topics of each of your pieces of content, you need to use your own best practices for providing the answers. Find out how your competitors are talking about these questions and do it better. Go to your internal subject matter experts and get their insights. Find the answers that align your domain expertise with customer needs.

This is the moment—when you've set your strategy and chosen your keywords and questions, but before your writers start to work—to bring in your experts and your internal domain expertise. Because you are not writing just any answer to customers' questions. You are writing the answer that draws them toward what you have to offer.

This is also why we believe it's critical to your success with PBM that your writers are also educated on the best practices we're covering in this chapter. Building a data-driven Pillar Strategy and then farming out the content creation through a low-cost freelance website won't work. Investing in your writers so that they also become fluent in the PBM approach is how you create content that is truly aligned to your customers' needs and wins you Page One rankings.

As an aside, this is also why trusting AI content-generation tools simply won't work for PBM. While there are some applications of this nascent tech that make a lot of sense—like email copy, for example—the tightrope dance of utilizing keywords in the exact right way to speak to customer context is simply too much for any modern AI writing tool to handle.

USE THOSE QUESTIONS IN CONTENT HEADINGS

This is a simple point but a powerful one: once you have chosen questions to build your content around, use those questions as the subheadings in the content—and in the H2 heading tags.

Most websites are designed to assign headers and header tags to separate content on the page. Usually, H1 headings are titles, while H2 headings are section headers within the text. These section heads provide a quality user experience by allowing readers to skim directly to the information they are interested in. If they reflect the questions the reader searched for and wants answered, she will see the content as relevant and engage more deeply.

Because of this, search engines pay attention to headings and heading tags, especially H2 headings and tags. As a bonus, if you provide great answers to questions customers are entering when they search, your answers may well end up in the featured snippets (which we often refer to as "answer boxes") on search engines. Since those answer boxes show up very close to the top of the search results and are popular with searchers, they represent a powerful opportunity for visibility and engagement.

PBM IN PRACTICE

Going back to our earlier example of Jennifer's Sub-Pillar Page titled, "Free Document Generation Software," here's a final look at the outline Jennifer prepared for her writer using the keywords and questions she selected from DemandJump's Content Brief tool.

H1: Free Document Generation Software

Introduction: Free document generation software is available in abundance—but it's not without its limitations. In this guide, we'll explore your options for free automated document generation tools and how to find the right one for your needs. We'll also take a look at what you could be missing out on if you limit yourself to what's free.

H2: What is automated document generation?

Keywords to include in this section:

- Document generation tools
- Automated documents
- What is integrated document generation?

H2: What is document generation software?

Keywords to include in this section:

- Document generation software
- Word program for Windows 10

H2: Is there free document generation software?

Keywords to include in this section:

- Free document editing apps for Android
- Document editing software free download
- Free document automation software

H2: What should I expect from a free document generation tool?

Keywords to include in this section:

- Document generation software features

H2: What is the best free document generator?

Keywords to include in this section:

- Best free document generation software
- Top free document automation tools

Conclusion: Highlight the advanced workflow and integration features of paid solutions. Don't mention EasySigner by name, but point out what paid tiers can provide, then work organically towards a "try it free" CTA for EasySigner.

Guided by questions used as H2s, Jennifer was able to sort keywords she wanted to target under each one, aligned to actual real-world customer behavior, and provide an overall flow for this article for her writer. Without this guidance from the spiderweb, Jennifer's writer probably wouldn't have even considered writing about apps for Android—but now they know it's a relevant, important topic to cover.

INCLUDE PILLAR AND SUB-PILLAR TOPIC TITLES IN YOUR CONTENT

The final element of high-impact content creation is including the titles of other pieces of content in each of your articles. We will talk more in the next chapter about how and when to use these references as links. The key here is to remember that all references should point "upward" in your content pyramid.

In other words, every Sub-Pillar Page and Supporting Blog should include the title of the main Pillar Page somewhere in the text because the Pillar Page is at the top of the content pyramid. Similarly, a Supporting Blog could include the title of the Sub-Pillar Page it is connected to, moving the reader upward through the pyramid.

This upward-linking structure reflects how people search. They tend to start by looking for specific, detailed answers to immediate problems, and as they find out more, they broaden their search to fill in gaps in their knowledge about the larger topic. Offering them the opportunity to broaden their search within your own content keeps them engaging on your site instead of going elsewhere.

THE PLATFORM

Our goal in this book is to show you how exponentially more effective your content marketing can be using the principles and methodologies of Pillar-Based Marketing, and how to apply those principles and methodologies in your own work.

As you may be starting to see, the ability to visualize and align with the spiderweb of real-world search behaviors is powerful and game-changing—but very hard to do manually. That's why, when we choose Pillar Topics and create Pillar Strategies for B2B and B2C customers, we use our machine-learning tools to generate and prioritize the spiderweb.

And when our writers set out to create individual pieces of content, they use a tool called the Content Brief, which is a multifaceted report that shows them exactly the questions to address in each article, what audiences want to know about each question, and how to structure the content to provide the best experience for the reader.

The principles of PBM above can work for anyone, in any industry, and we've seen companies make powerful improvements in their rankings just by applying and leveraging the principles we've laid out here. But throughout the book, you'll see that we have used our tool as the example for how to apply these principles. For now, our platform is the only tool we know of that can automate the process and provide three-dimensional insight across the whole network. We're clearly biased, but with results like the ones we've come to expect from PBM strategies powered by our technology, why wouldn't we be?

THE TAKEAWAY

Writing content is where theory meets practice. It's where the principles of PBM take shape in actual articles, blogs, and web pages. In the past, the writing process has been mysterious and somewhat nerve-racking. Faced with the blank page and a general topic to write about, what exactly do you say? How does a writer know if they are addressing the concerns of greatest interest to readers? How should they organize an article to both provide a great reading experience and maximize page rankings?

As with every other step in the content marketing process, content writing can be demystified using data. Once again, put aside everything you think you know about keywords and SEO and instead build high-quality answers to the questions searchers are asking, connected within a network of related content.

Once you have that content, it's time to publish. It turns out there's an exponentially more powerful way to do that, too.

CHAPTER 10

PUBLISHING YOUR PILLAR CONTENT

Over at EasySigner, Jennifer is relieved. She's chosen her Pillar Topic, designed her strategy, and written her content, and now the content has been approved. It's ready to publish to the web any time she wants. The finish line on this campaign is so close she can feel it.

If she were approaching this campaign in the traditional way, she would now start to piece out her content according to her editorial calendar, publishing one or two pieces this week, then another piece next week, and so on, according to whatever schedule she's laid out. But we threw out the editorial calendar in Chapter 9. Instead of scheduling pieces to publish one at a time, we've built a network of interrelated, mutually supportive content that all works together to teach search engines that you are an authority on a particular topic.

Maximizing the impact and value of that network requires a

new approach to publishing. It turns out that the speed, order, and timing of publication all matter. How you link your content together, how you tell search engines that your content is available—every element of the publishing process impacts your rankings and how fast you can achieve them. Arbitrarily deciding on a timeline or schedule for release won't work; you need to know how to "go live" in a way that drives immediate impact and draws the attention of search engines to all your content at once.

In this chapter, we're going to show you how to turn all your conventional wisdom about content publishing on its head. Instead of spacing out your content for consistency, you're going to publish it all at once for maximum impact. Instead of choosing what to publish next based on coverage across topics, you're going to publish your content pyramid from the top down. And instead of trying to link every piece to every other piece, you're going to teach search engines about your network by linking upward through your pyramid.

THE FUNDAMENTALS

The key to the entire PBM approach is the network, and publishing your content is no different. For that network to do its job—to signal to search engines that you are an authority on your Pillar Topic—it can't be dribbled out piecemeal over weeks or months.

> The network has to be a network from the beginning, from the moment you publish. The network effect only works when all the pieces are live and working together.

PUBLISH THE NETWORK, NOT THE PIECES

Every step in the PBM process is about the network. Choosing a Pillar Topic is about identifying the hub, the powerful search term you'll construct your network around. Building your Pillar Strategy is about recreating a version of the real-world search network on your own domain. And writing your content is about making each piece a powerful contributor to that network in its own right. If you were now to take that network and publish it in the traditional way—one piece to start, another piece in a week or two—you would be undoing all the work you've done to build it in the first place.

Publishing your entire network together, as a single unit, ensures that your content creates the immediate impact you designed it to create.

To some people, this approach can seem slower rather than faster. If you have one or two pieces of content finished and approved, wouldn't you rank faster by publishing those pieces now, rather than waiting for all the others to be finished?

Surprisingly, no.

Because each piece in the network reinforces and supports all the others, publishing piecemeal means you lose the synergistic effect of the combined content. The underlying idea behind the content network is that the whole is greater than the parts. We've seen this over and over: every piece performs better individually when it's part of the interrelated whole. We've built PBM around the network concept because the data shows us that modern search engines respond to the entirety of the content on your site, not just individual pieces.

It may feel good to publish a piece as soon as it's ready, but it pays to hold off.

Whatever the reason, the data is clear: velocity in publishing PBM content plays a role in earning top rankings quickly.

In the next section, we'll talk in detail about the best order in which to publish your 16 pieces of content to create the network effect fast and with the maximum impact. We'll show you how to use links to teach search engines how your content is related. And we'll discuss how images and limited paid strategies can help kick-start your rankings by bringing traffic to your site right away. But the key throughout is the same: your publishing strategy should be about building the network, because the network effect, not the individual piece of content, drives traffic and rankings.

WHAT YOU DON'T NEED

We don't like to focus on the negative, but there are so many misconceptions out there about how to effectively publish content that we felt we needed to address a couple of them.

First of all, you don't need backlinks for PBM to work its magic. A backlink occurs when someone else on the internet links to your content. Early in the history of SEO, search engines did respond to backlinks—so much so that SEO experts were abusing the system. They would create entire domains solely for the purpose of linking back to their own content. They would spam other sites' comment sections with links to their blogs. That's not organic engagement, and search engines no longer validate it.

That's not to say that backlinks can't be valuable today. Many SEO experts exert a lot of time and effort on backlinking strategies that help to prop up content and lend it more authority. The benefits of this are undeniable, albeit hard-won. However, this work in no way drives a better user experience. And, from what we've seen, it's a slower way to build honest-to-goodness authority in the eyes of search engines.

You should use links to create the network effect among your pieces of content and show search engines (not convince them, but *show* them) that you are an authentic authority on your Pillar Topic. Backlinks are not part of that strategy. If someone authentically likes your content and links to it, all the better. If the entity that links to your content is itself an authority on the topic—such as the Mayo Clinic linking to your content on a particular disease or drug—that might have some significant impact on your search engine rankings. Otherwise, backlinks as an SEO strategy pale in comparison to the speed and ranking power of PBM.

We know backlinks don't matter in the world of PBM because we have maintained no backlinking strategy of any kind to drive the results described in this book.

So, you tell us: would you rather focus your time and energy emailing strangers to propose link swaps, or would you rather put that effort toward writing the content your customers actually care about and get to Page One on your own? We know what our answer would be every time.

Second, you don't need domain authority. Domain authority is a grading system that search engines assign to your entire domain, reflecting how authoritative that domain is on certain topics. It essentially says, "This is a good website," and it's often a reflection of how long you've been publishing and how much total content you have.

Domain authority is nice to have. If you have a high domain authority score, that's probably good for your overall traffic. But it doesn't predict how well any particular content you write will generate traffic, and it certainly doesn't predict whether that content will generate sales or leads or revenue around the product or service you are trying to promote. More to the point, it's just not necessary. The network effect, when used correctly, replaces the need for domain authority. A complete Pillar Strategy, with the 16 pieces of content you've developed through this process, signals to search engines that you are now an authority on this particular, specific Pillar Topic more effectively than a high score for your overall website.

We don't just think this is true; we know it. For example, one of our customers came to us with a domain authority of four. For those who don't know about domain authority, the highest possible number is 100, and the lowest is zero. Four is so low that it's practically nonexistent. The customer was concerned that their low domain authority meant they could never rank above their larger competitors for the topics they cared about. We worked with this customer to develop their content network and published it using the approach outlined in this chapter, and in a couple of weeks, they were outranking competitors with domain authority scores of 50 and higher on the topics they wanted to own.

Not too surprisingly, this company's domain authority went up over time as well. We see that a lot: a well-designed Pillar-based content network will help improve your domain authority. But it doesn't work the other way. A high domain authority score won't guarantee you Page One rankings or drive revenue from your content.

This is why when we talk about "authority" in the world of PBM, we aren't talking about domain authority. We're talking about *topical* authority—the only kind that truly matters if you want to drive remarkable marketing outcomes.

Don't worry. We're not asking you to totally give up the strategies you are comfortable with. If you want to add backlinks or build your domain authority later, go ahead. As far as we know today, those efforts may help in the long run. But for now, just think about all the time and effort you save by not bothering with tasks that don't contribute to the outsized results the PBM methodology offers.

PBM IN ACTION

None of the action points in this chapter are rocket science, but every one of them will substantially increase not only your rankings on search engines but the speed with which you achieve those rankings. You don't want to expend the time, effort, and resources to develop a data-driven, customer-aligned content network, only to lose steam in the publication process. The best practices below will ensure that your publication strategy maximizes the impact of your content and that you have the infrastructure in place to make your content searchable and rankable.

THE VELOCITY FACTOR

We mentioned this in the previous selection, but it's worth mentioning again: the goal of PBM is to recreate the network of real-world search behavior on your site, and no single piece of content can achieve that on its own. You need to publish the entire network in one push, over the course of just a few days.

So instead of publishing each piece separately on the basis of an editorial calendar, you will create all 16 initial pieces of the network (your Pillar Page, three Sub-Pillar Pages, and 12 Supporting Blogs), load them into the back end of your CMS, and wait. Think about it this way: if you publish 16 pieces of content over 16 weeks, it will take at least 16 weeks to get the full effect of the network, whereas if you publish over the course of a few days, you can start to see results immediately.

Time and again we've seen that publishing the entire network has exponential benefits in terms of both rankings and speed; in some cases, customers see Page One rankings in a matter of days or even hours once the entire network is up.

However, while you want to get the entire network up and working together as quickly as possible, you can't publish all 16 pieces simultaneously. You have to start from the hub.

LINK FROM THE BOTTOM UP

You have your completed content queued up. It's ready to go—but it's still not a complete network. A network is not just a collection of individual items; it is also a system of interconnections among those items. Those interconnections are your links. All roads through your content should lead upward to the Pillar Page.

This is where a lot of content writers get hung up. In their experience, linking is about creating as many connections and callbacks among pieces of content as possible. They want to link every piece to every other piece. That's not wrong, per se. If you want to link across Sub-Pillars and among Supporting Blogs, our data suggests that isn't going to hurt your network effect, especially if the links make sense organically in the piece you're writing, rather than being forced.

What makes the difference in terms of ranking, though, is linking upward.

> The question you should be asking yourself is "Are we reinforcing the network effect with our linking?"

We have studied the data on thousands of pieces of content, and it's clear that the most important function of links in Pillar Content is establishing the hierarchy of your network. Your network is built as a pyramid, with the Pillar Page at the top and the Supporting Blogs at the bottom. To establish the hierarchy of that content, links should point upward. Supporting Blogs should link up to the Sub-Pillars they are connected to, which should in turn link up to the Pillar Page. Furthermore, the links establish the hierarchy most effectively when you use the exact article titles as the links. So each Supporting Blog, for example, should contain the title of the related Sub-Pillar post as a link, and each Sub-Pillar post should contain the title of your Pillar Page as a link.

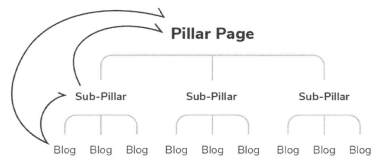

Each Supporting Blog post should link up to both the Pillar Page and, if applicable, the Sub-Pillar Page it falls under in the Pillar Strategy, using the titles of those pieces as anchor text. All Sub-Pillar Pages should link up to the Pillar Page in the same way. This methodology recreates the spiderweb network of actual real-world customer behavior and how keywords and questions are related to one another.

Linking upward recreates what the data shows to be the most organic, and most common, search experience. When a person wants to explore a topic, they generally start with a very specific question—usually a problem they are trying to solve right now. Then, as they continue to search and to learn more about their problem and its possible solutions, they tend to broaden their scope. Your Pillar Content follows this same structure, with the Supporting Blogs at the bottom addressing specific, immediate questions and concerns and the Pillar Page at the top providing information about the broad category topic. Linking upward mirrors readers' real-world search strategies, leading them organically through your content in the order most useful to them—and most likely to keep them on your site.

Take EasySigner as an example. Most people—even those who need document generation software—don't start by searching "document generation." *That's where they end up.* Where they start might be "how do I create a document online?" or "where can I create a document online?" or some other related question. These questions show up in EasySigner's Supporting Blogs because EasySigner discovered them in their spiderweb data, back in the content creation step. In fact, EasySigner's Supporting Blogs now offer some of the best content on the internet around these specific, common customer questions, meaning that readers find themselves on the EasySigner blog posts early in their buying journey. As they read, they become curious to see more examples of document generation—and there is a convenient link to a Sub-Pillar Page on "examples of document generation." Readers engage organically with the upward links on EasySigner's page because they mirror their real-world search process.

In short, linking upward makes the content network on your site feel natural and meaningful to customers and leads them organically toward your sales or lead generation points. Any other link you add, such as a link from a Sub-Pillar Page to a Supporting Blog that goes into more detail on a topic, is just gravy—and a good user experience.

PUBLISH FROM THE TOP DOWN

Your content strategy translates the hub and spokes of the real-world search network into a pyramid, where the Pillar Page corresponds to the hub of the network, and all the other Sub-Pillar Pages and Supporting Blogs correspond to the branches out from that center. For the elements of the network to work together as intended, the top of the pyramid has to be published first, and then the rest of the content from the top down. Otherwise, the supporting content has nothing to connect to.

So your first job in publishing your Pillar Content is to publish

your core Pillar Page and make sure that it is indexed before going live with any of your other pieces.

Let's talk for a minute about indexing because it's a simple step, but you cannot get any organic traffic to a piece of content until that piece of content is indexed. Without traffic, you cannot rank. Indexing is that important.

All search engines maintain what is essentially a map of the entire internet: all the content, all the links, and all the data related to each page on the web. That is the index. Until your page or site is indexed, the search engine can't and won't collect any data on it. This means that any traffic your page gets before it's indexed won't affect your rankings. Your Pillar Page could attract hundreds of hits through paid channels, but if it's not indexed, none of those hits will count toward your ranking.

Fortunately, indexing is not complicated. There are tools you can use to get your site indexed quickly; you don't have to wait for it to happen organically. We use Google Search Console, but you can use whatever tool you have access to. Most of these tools allow you to request indexing for a new piece of content, then notify you when the page is indexed.

Once your Pillar Page is published and indexed, you can go ahead and begin publishing your other content, from the top down, recreating the hubs and spoke elements of the network. You will publish and index your Sub-Pillar Pages, then your Supporting Blogs, ensuring that each level is indexed before you publish the next level down.

We usually manage to complete this process in three days,

publishing and indexing the Pillar Page one day, the Sub-Pillar Pages the next, and then the Supporting Blogs.

If you are proactive about indexing, you can get all your content live within a matter of days. If your site is well-built and you really want to maximize your impact, you can keep a close eye on Google Search Console and, the moment you know your Pillar Page has indexed, publish the Sub-Pillars, then do the same for each Supporting Blog.

In brief, the order of operations for publishing your content should be as follows:

- Wait until all 16 initial Pillar Content pieces are complete and approved.
- Ensure that all links are active and that all Sub-Pillar and Supporting Blog pages link upward.
- Publish your core Pillar Page and request indexing.
- Once your Pillar Page is live and indexed, publish your Sub-Pillar Pages and request indexing.
- Once your Sub-Pillar Pages are indexed, publish your Supporting Blogs and request indexing.

GET YOUR HOUSE IN ORDER

Unfortunately, even if you do everything we've outlined here to maximize the impact of your content, your publication process can be stalled or derailed by back-end issues on your own site. In some cases, these issues can keep your site from being ranked at all. The fixes below aren't particularly difficult or time-consuming, but together they can have a substantial effect on your content's visibility to search engines.

The first cleanup job involves your sitemap. The sitemap is the page that lists all the content on your website, usually in a hierarchy or flowchart. If you don't have a sitemap, search engines cannot index your site, and as we mentioned before, if your site is not indexed, no data is collected for it, which means that even if you get thousands of engagements, your rankings won't improve. Take the time to ensure that you have a sitemap and that it is up to date.

Also, make sure you only have one. We've been surprised more than once to find that companies—especially larger companies with older sites or those that have gone through multiple site upgrades—have two or three or even more sitemaps. Sometimes, no one at the company knows these multiple maps even exist. Multiple sitemaps will confuse search engines, and if search engines can't understand the hierarchy of your site, they won't index it, and you won't be able to rank. Have a sitemap, update it, and make sure it's your only one.

The second cleanup job involves loading speeds. Slow loading speeds will cause search engines to down-rank, or even ignore, your site. Do your research: find out what loading speeds are acceptable for different kinds of content in your industry (video, text blog posts, etc.) and work with your IT team to ensure that your site is loading at the industry standard or better. Developing exceptional content only to have it remain unsearchable because of slow loading speeds would be a tragedy. Find out who in your organization is responsible for this and verify it before you publish.

Finally, make sure that your content is mobile-friendly. A huge percentage of searches take place on mobile devices, so a mobile-friendly site will generate more traffic overall, which is an easy win. But there's more to it than that. Because modern search engines are trying first and foremost to create an engaging experience for searchers, they prioritize sites and content that are accessible to all users, including mobile users. Most website hosting platforms today offer mobile-friendly responsive designs. Use them.

Having all of these pieces in place will ensure that your publishing and indexing go smoothly and quickly, which means that search engines can start gathering the data that will get you to Page One.

USE ORIGINAL IMAGES

Part of publishing your written content is deciding what to publish with it, whether that's images, videos, calls to action, etc. Creating original video, for example, can give you huge gains in rankings. Just recently, Google changed its algorithms so that videos can show up on the results page with the company's domain name, rather than YouTube's domain, even if the videos are hosted on YouTube. If your company has the resources to create and include high-quality videos, go for it.

But don't worry; you don't have to shoot video or host a You-Tube channel (although if you do, including video content on your PBM pages can only help your rankings). All you have to do is use original, unique images.

> We've said it many times, and we'll say it again because it's so important: modern search engines don't just care what keywords you use. They care that you are creating a good reader experience.

Creating a good experience means engaging different kinds of learners and different kinds of audiences. Adding pictures and infographics does that work—but only if the images are unique. Search engines don't see stock images as valuable. As far as the search engine is concerned, if you used a stock image, you didn't add anything to the overall content of the internet, which means you are not offering something new that will truly engage readers.

Fortunately, search engines aren't looking for anything complicated. Your images can be very simple, as long as they're custom.

We've seen content improve in the rankings just by adding a pull quote in graphic format. You don't even need a graphic designer to create that kind of image; your writers can do it on their own using a platform like Canva. If you have an original photo that works with the content, by all means, use that. Generate a simple infographic using a few pieces of data from the article. Offer a flowchart of the main topics or a pull-out example formatted as an image. None of these ideas take more than a few minutes to generate, but search engines will see them as original, engaging content—and reward them as such.

And if you take the time to write real alt text (the back-end description of the image) that describes what's in the image and also uses the title keyword of the piece of content it's used in, that's just one more opportunity to earn a top ranking.

KICK-START WITH PAID STRATEGIES

You're in the home stretch now. You've got your content pyramid published, indexed, and linked. Your website is in order and searchable. Each piece of content includes at least one simple, custom graphic to signal to the world that it's new and original. You've hit "go," and everything is live. Now is the time to kick your traffic into high gear. And although everything we said about paid strategies is true—it can't give you an appreciating asset, you don't control it in the long run, and so on—it does have value as a means of jump-starting your ascent to Page One.

All of this goes back to the key point about modern search engines: they no longer look at the content itself as their main way of determining what's good and what's not. Sure, they look at keywords and backlinks and all that. But the most important signal of quality for modern search engines is engagement on a post, and the only way to get engagement, to draw the attention of the search engines, is to get traffic.

Because you have written your content to align with topics customers care about, it won't take much for search engines to see its value. Customers will want to engage with it, and that will drive your traffic in the long run. It's absolutely possible to get that engagement organically, without any paid strategies, but if you want to kick into high gear very quickly, you can apply a small, limited budget for paid traffic to each piece of content and get immediate results.

We've seen customers achieve big gains spending as little as $10 on each piece of content, but the sweet spot is around $40–$50 each. You can use this strategy on whatever outlet you usually use to drive qualified traffic, whether that's Facebook or LinkedIn or some other platform. If you have a solid paid search strategy in place already, you can drive paid traffic on Google, or if you use a content syndication platform like Outbrain, you can use that. It doesn't matter, as long as you effectively target the primary customer that you want to reach with your specific Pillar Topic.

Just a tiny amount of qualified, paid traffic is enough to drive real engagement, as long as you've developed your content the way we have taught you here. Once people start clicking onto your new content, search engines will see it and start evaluating it, and that will kick-start your rankings. This is exactly how we've gotten to Page One in a matter of days or even hours for customers across industries, organizations, and topics.

To reiterate: a paid strategy is not necessary. You can absolutely get to Page One without it. But assigning even a tiny budget for paid strategy *once you already have your entire content network up and indexed* can substantially accelerate your results. This is just one way that PBM extends to elements of your marketing strategy beyond content alone; it can even begin to inform your paid strategy to increase the value of your organic content assets.

THE TAKEAWAY

If you want to know just how fast and powerful this publication strategy is, consider the competitive landscape around COVID-19 over the past two years. Overnight, a set of terms and topics that had never even existed before became the most sought-after on the internet.

In 2020, we were working with a customer in the pharmaceutical business. This customer was a research organization; they were not in the business of disease testing at all. Their primary business was to collect samples of novel diseases for pharmaceutical companies to use in developing treatments. As part of their normal course of business isolating COVID-19 samples, they created a quick and effective way to test for COVID-19 very early on in the pandemic. In light of the dire need at the time, the US government literally begged them to develop and sell the test for broad consumer use. They agreed.

As far as marketing the test, though, they didn't know where to start. This was an entirely new space for them—a market they weren't familiar with at all—so they came to us to develop new content to promote the test. They were concerned because they had no content on any related topics anywhere on their site, and they didn't know if they could get anyone to notice them.

We went through the PBM process with them, selecting their Pillar Topic, developing their strategy, and writing the content. While our writers worked, we collaborated with the customer to build an entirely new blog around this new topic on a subdomain of their main site. Then we went live, exactly as we've outlined here, with all their Pillar Content over the course of a few days.

In less than four hours after we went live, their site was seeing organic traffic around the keyword "COVID-19 testing," possibly the most competitive keyword to exist at the time. They got to Page One overnight not just for one term but for dozens. People lined up around the block at their testing sites, they ended up making millions in revenue on a product that wasn't even part of their core business, and tens of thousands of individuals got tested for a potentially deadly disease.

There is no possible way they could have had such results

with any traditional content publication strategy. If they had attempted to parse out an article about COVID-19 testing one week, then a description of their product features the next week, and so on, it would have taken them months to gain any traction at all. Only creating the network based on real-world search behavior and then publishing that network simultaneously, in one push, creates the kind of overnight upset in search rankings and customer behavior that changes the world.

Which means there are only two questions left: how, exactly, do you keep track of all this success, and how do you keep it going?

CHAPTER 11

MEASURING YOUR IMPACT

Over the past ten years or so, as marketing has become increasingly data-driven, marketers have developed dozens of metrics to evaluate the performance of their content and, ideally, predict their next steps. Some have looked at impressions or click rates. Others have been more interested in ROI, measuring the cost per campaign or per click. Many have focused on overall traffic, assuming that lots of eyes on the content will lead to lots of sales or leads.

None of these are bad metrics; all of them tell you something about how your content is performing. But as we have seen, the key to generating revenue through content marketing is to reach Page One—and the key to reaching Page One is organic alignment to customer needs. In other words, the most important metrics are those that tell you whether audiences like what they see. If readers see your content as valuable, they will engage with it, and search engines will rank it highly. Similarly, if search engines rank your content highly, customers will find it—and if it is valuable, they will engage with it. Together, rankings and engagement create a growth cycle that drives sales and leads.

So the metrics you choose should, at a minimum, allow you to quantify and prove those two outcomes: high search engine rankings and above-average customer engagement with your content.

But truly powerful metrics do more than just tell you how you're doing: they show you what to do next. Where to grow your content, what new topics to take on, and how to tweak your network to overtake specific competitors. Whatever you measure should tell you not only what seems to have been working so far, or what worked in the past, but how to continue improving.

THE FUNDAMENTALS

Successful content has two jobs. First, it has to draw people to your site as they pursue their buying journeys out on the internet. Whether they are individuals looking to make immediate purchases or corporate committees seeking solutions to enterprise-wide problems, potential customers need to be encountering your content at each point along their path to a decision. Great content brings potential customers to you.

Second, your content needs to keep people on your site once they find it. If readers click onto your content only to bounce off it again, or if they never click through to another page in your network, your content isn't working. Great content keeps readers engaged with you until they are ready to purchase.

The two critical metrics we'll cover in this chapter show you how your content is performing on these two jobs.

RANKING

For your content to bring customers to you, they have to find it. It's that simple.

Increases in traffic to your site—that is, increases in the number of people who have visited a particular page or piece of content—can tell you that more people are finding you and that one piece of content has drawn more attention than another. That can be valuable information. But traffic can't tell you how to bring more customers to your site.

In the first place, traffic data reflects what has happened in the past. It shows you how many people have come to your site recently, or since you posted new content, or over time. You can find out if the number of people coming to a particular page has increased, but you don't know whether that trend will continue—or why it happened.

Traffic metrics can't tell you the most important pieces of information: how and why customers found you. If the traffic to a particular page on your site increases, that's great. If you placed a paid ad, you might be able to see how many of the new visitors came directly through that ad. You can't see why any particular individual clicked on that ad, whether they would click on similar ads in the future, or which other people might be attracted by the same ad.

Traffic data also can't tell you how much of the total you own. Even if you see your traffic on a particular page increase by 10% over a particular week, you still don't know the maximum amount of traffic you could have hoped to achieve. You can't know whether your content is truly successful if you don't know whether the traffic you are getting represents 50% of the total available market for your topic, or only 5%. Traffic data for your site tells you how much you have but not how much there is.

Ranking data fills in these gaps because ranking data shows you not only how you rank overall but how you rank for each specific term, question, or topic, and how each individual piece of content in your network ranks for each of those terms, questions, and topics. There's no guesswork about why one paid ad was successful and another wasn't, or what sparked customer interest in your content in a given week. You know precisely how and why they came to you, and how and why they are coming to each specific piece of content.

Ranking data also shows you the percentage of the total available market you are attracting. Since you already know the size of the potential market for each term or topic you used in your content (having analyzed the total competitive landscape for each term when you built your Pillar Strategy), you can immediately evaluate how much of the total you are garnering. You can compare your rankings with competitors' rankings on the same topics to immediately understand not only where you stand right now but whether you are gaining or losing ground. Even if you're not yet at number one for a particular topic, moving up the rankings proves that your ability to bring in new traffic over time is increasing. That is powerful.

Finally, ranking data is predictive. Consistently hitting Page One, or even better, position one on Page One, for a particular topic or question means that your content will *continue* to drive traffic. Seeing the full list of terms and search questions that brought customers to each of your individual pieces of content means that you can predict exactly where new, additional customers are likely to come from.

When we track Pillar Content metrics with customers, we start with ranking data. Specifically, we start with trends. We don't focus at first on absolute ranking numbers but on progress over time. Successful content isn't just about achieving a certain rank or number of rankings in a certain amount of time but about improving your ranking—in particular, gaining rank in comparison to your competitors. The best way to know that is to look at how your Page One rankings are performing on a week-by-week basis, how individual terms and Pillar Topics you've selected are performing each week, and which specific position each individual piece of content in the network is achieving each week. You should also track how your Page One through Page Ten rankings are performing week over week because that way, you can see your content moving upward through the competitive landscape even if it's not yet on Page One.

The key pieces of information here are the trends and the comparisons: whether your content, your topics, and your overall site are moving up or down in rankings, and whether you are gaining ground on competitors in areas you care about.

It's also important to track not only how you are ranking for the individual Pillar Topics and Sub-Pillar Topics you've selected, but how your site and content are trending overall. Remember how we talked about each piece of content in the network supporting all the others? This is where you get to see that happening. As you increase your rankings for one topic or article, you'll see each of the items in the network—and even topics and pieces of content on your site that aren't part of this specific Pillar Topic network—increasing as well.

Later in this chapter, we'll talk about how to use your ranking data to drive continuous improvement in your content. But first, let's discuss how to determine whether your content is doing its other job—keeping customers on your site once they've found you.

ENGAGEMENT

It's great to have increased rankings and the increased traffic that goes along with them, but for your content to generate leads or sales, customers must find your content compelling enough to stay. That's why, in addition to ranking data, you need to be gathering metrics on engagement.

Specifically, you should be looking at the average time spent on each page, the exit percentage from each page, and the bounce rate. Together, these three data points provide a detailed picture of how valuable your audience finds your content and how likely they are to stay on your site once they've found it.

Time on Page

"Time on page," the average time spent by visitors to each specific page of your website, is the most important metric for measuring engagement.

In 2021, the internet average for time on page was 52 seconds, although the average is much lower for the vast majority of content, while a few popular or authoritative sites skew the average upward. Before 2021, the average was even lower, hovering closer to 30 seconds for the previous few years. The averages trend somewhat longer or shorter across industries but are under a minute in almost every field. In other words, most readers spend very little time on any individual web page.

Although many marketers do look at the average "time on page" data for their industry, they tend to respond to it backward. Instead of writing more engaging content that readers want to engage with longer, they revise their content to be shorter, to make it readable in the average time. Many even provide "estimated reading times" to reassure readers that they won't have to spend long reading an article.

Cutting down your content to match average reading times is not effective. You cannot fully answer a reader's questions or address their concerns in 30 seconds. If you can't hold a reader's attention longer than that, your content is not providing them the answers they are looking for. You might have gotten a data point—a click-through or an impression or a website hit—but you have not gotten engagement.

The good news is that we have all been vastly underestimating internet users. Average time on page is not low because people don't want to read, or because their attention spans are short, as some proponents of short content will tell you. Average time on page is low because the average internet user is savvy, is focused, and knows what they are looking for. If you provide content that aligns with their needs, they will stay.

> Readers will stay on your page as long as they feel they are getting value. If they are interested in what they're reading, or if they feel that they're getting answers to the questions they care about, they will read as much as you can write. When readers like what they see and stay on the page, *that* is engagement.

How do we know that readers are savvy and that their attention spans aren't the problem? Data from the thousands of blog posts published by PBM practitioners.

When we write Supporting Blogs (generally about 750 words), the average time on page is 2 and a half minutes. That's more than two and a half times the internet average for all content, and it's our shortest format. For Sub-Pillar posts, which run around 2,000 words, our average is 5 minutes and 53 seconds. Nearly six times the internet average. Some of our Pillar Pages, at 3,000 words or more, have achieved averages of 14 or 15 minutes.

Customers are spending *15 minutes* on a single page of content—more than 15 times the internet average. Attention span is not the issue. Writing relevant content is.

Fortunately, your content doesn't need to hit these numbers to get substantially above-average engagement. If you write your content to directly address the needs and questions of customers based on the real-world search data, as we've shown you how to do, the time customers are spending on your page will be higher than the industry average—and higher than your competitors. Even a slight edge in engagement over other content on a given topic will be enough to drive substantial increases in leads and sales.

If you are seeing a higher-than-average time on page across all of your content, with the longest times recorded on your Pillar Page, you know that your content is driving the kind of deep engagement you want.

Exit Percentage and Bounce Rate

Exit percentage and bounce rate are closely related metrics that also help you measure your readers' engagement with your content. Neither is as telling as time on page, but together, they give you a sense of whether an individual piece of content is working to keep readers on your site or prompting them to go elsewhere.

Exit percentage measures the number of visitors who leave your site after looking at a particular page. If you are on a website, and you're reading a blog post, and something in that post (or something that's missing from it) makes you want to leave that site, the content on that page is not doing its job. A low exit percentage, in other words, confirms that a particular page is providing readers with enough value to want to stay, and it lets you know that readers who engage with you through that page are likely to click through to other content on your site. If your exit percentage for a particular piece of content goes down, especially if it goes down compared to other pages on your site, you know that it is performing well.

Bounce rate is similar but more specific: it measures the percentage of your audience that leaves your site after viewing only this one page of content. Whereas exit percentage may capture readers who spent half an hour on your site and finally happened to leave after reading a particular page, bounce rate looks only at those readers who saw this one piece, didn't like it, and left immediately.

To generate sales, leads, and revenue—to contribute to the organization's bottom line—content has to bring customers to you and keep them on your site long enough to learn what you can offer them. There are lots of metrics available to marketers, but ranking and engagement are the strongest signals you have that your content is doing what you designed it to do.

PBM IN ACTION

Once you have collected all this data, your final step is to determine, "What next?" For most of marketing history, getting to the end of a campaign was a moment of panic because it meant starting the entire process over again, back at guesswork and wishful thinking. When you don't know what works or doesn't work, there's no clear way to know which way to pivot next. Should you do more of what you're doing and hope it continues to work? Should you change strategies? Try to reach a different audience? Even if your existing content has been doing exceptionally well, if you don't know why it's working or how you did it, you don't know how to build on it.

As we promised at the beginning of this chapter, we're going to show you exactly how to use the data you've gathered to make confident, strategic decisions about your next steps. Specifically, we're going to talk about three options for moving forward: you can work on a brand-new Pillar, expand your first pillar with new content, or update your existing Pillar Content to make it richer. These options are not mutually exclusive. As you continue to evaluate your current content performance and your ongoing business needs, you will probably do some version of all three of these, often at the same time.

WORK ON A NEW PILLAR

One option is to start the process over again with a new Pillar Topic, going back to the "Choose a Pillar Topic" step and developing 16 new pieces around a different core term or concept.

You should choose this option if you've gotten excellent results from your first Pillar Topic. For example, if you've overtaken your competition on the terms that matter to you most, gotten Page One rankings on those terms, feel comfortable with the amount of new traffic you're creating, and think that the amount and quality of new traffic aligns with the investment you made in that original Pillar Topic, you are ready to put your initial pillar in maintenance mode and start building a new one.

You might also choose to work on a new Pillar Topic if your company offers different types of features, services, or products, or wants to reach new markets or industries. If your business plan involves growing in multiple different directions at once or prioritizes gaining market share across a variety of different industries, you might gain more value from multiple Pillar Topics than from continually improving on one. In this case, you should develop a new Pillar Topic around one of your other products or feature sets, or around a term of interest to a specific industry you want to reach.

PBM IN PRACTICE

Jennifer at EasySigner has been evaluating the metrics from her first pillar, "document generation," and she is pleased with what she's seeing. EasySigner's content is now ranking on Page One for the "document generation" search term, engagement with almost every piece of content is far above the industry average, and her Pillar Page is driving substantial new business to her lead generation page. But she remembers, from her initial data analysis, that the search term "electronic signature" was also highly connected in her network. She chooses to create a new pillar and starts the process from the beginning around that term.

At DemandJump, we've chosen to create new Pillar Topics many times over. As our pillar around the term "content marketing" has started to perform exceptionally well, for example, we've expanded to include pillars around "SEO pillar," "Pillar-Based Marketing," "keyword research," and "website content," among others. Like a lot of startups, we've found ourselves serving new markets and offering new services as we've grown, and we want to drive traffic to these new areas. Our new Pillar Topics reflect that growth.

In short, if you feel satisfied with the performance of your first Pillar Content, and your business priority is to reach new markets or build new product lines, creating a new pillar may be your best option.

EXPAND YOUR FIRST PILLAR WITH NEW CONTENT

Another option for your next step is to expand your existing pillar with new content, creating new pages to flesh out the content network around the initial Pillar Topic.

Expanding on your first pillar can be a good option if you are seeing that your initial content has performed well, but there's still a gap between the rankings you're getting and the rankings your competitors are getting. If you're in a highly competitive field or trying to own a highly competitive keyword, for example, you might find that you can't seem to dislodge larger competitors from the highest-level rankings.

As we mentioned in Chapter 8, 16 pieces of content is generally enough to get the results you want. In some cases, though, a pillar needs additional content in order to rank—like when DemandJump initially wrote 89 pieces of content to rank on Page One for "content marketing." So far, we've never seen another Pillar Topic that required anywhere near that level of additional content, but in some cases, adding a few new pieces can substantially increase your ability to capture pieces of your desired network that you missed initially. That said, since publishing that first batch of 89 pieces, we've added roughly 30 additional pieces of content to the interconnected "content marketing" Pillar Strategy.

In this case, you're going to go back to the content spiderweb you developed during your Pillar Strategy step and target Sub-Pillars and Supporting Blog topics you didn't cover in the initial content set. You will look at competitor data to determine the keywords your competitors are ranking for that you aren't, then go back to your spiderweb and find alignment. Where in the search data do those keywords overlap with your content network? Where can you build in new Sub-Pillars or Supporting Blogs to fill in those gaps and redirect your competitors' traffic to yourself?

What's so powerful about this option is that you will know

exactly what new content to write. There will be no guessing and wondering what you might have missed. The data will reveal the gaps and how to fill them.

UPGRADE YOUR EXISTING PILLAR CONTENT

The final option is to upgrade your existing Pillar Content to make it richer by revising existing Pillar Pages, Sub-Pillar Pages, or Supporting Blogs with new keywords, sections, headings, and so on.

This is often the best option to choose if your content originally performed well but then started to slip. Perhaps a particular Sub-Pillar Page or Supporting Blog was on Page One but isn't anymore. This tactic is particularly powerful if a piece of content is on the line between Page One and Page Two, ranking around number 11 or 12. Because such a large percentage of all traffic goes to pages on Page One, bumping a piece of content up one or two slots can mean the difference between no clicks at all and significant traffic.

The other benefit of this option is that it requires a relatively small investment. You can go back to the mini-spiderweb you developed during your content creation step and find keywords or questions you didn't originally include. Based on that data, you can add new sections (with new headers for the search engines to find), answer additional questions, or include new original graphics in your existing content.

> We see approximately 22% change in customer behavior year over year. This is a massive change in data and behavior year over year that marketers cannot keep up with unless they have a network-based AI content platform that automates identifying those changes. This means you will want to update roughly one-quarter of your content based on the current data on an ongoing basis to continue meeting changes in customer behavior. Instead of feeling overwhelmed by the steps you *could* take, you can now sleep well at night knowing you are ahead of the customer behavior change curve while your counterparts will be pulling out their hair trying to figure out why they still aren't driving results.

In fact, most of our customers end up coming back to this option regularly with all of their content because search engines want to see that you engage with and constantly update your content. Adding a new keyword or two, answering a new question, or replacing an older image can immediately bump up the rankings for a page that has slipped or is becoming stale.

Our own strategy reflects the value of this approach. In addition to the 30 or so new pieces we've added to the "content marketing" Pillar Strategy, we've also expanded and improved dozens of the original articles, working to maintain or increase rankings for keywords used in those pieces of content.

THE TAKEAWAY

One of the most incredible things about the PBM methodology—and by incredible, we mean we've literally had trouble believing it—is how often pieces of content we've created haven't needed to be touched for months or years. We watch the ranking and engagement metrics for every piece of content we create, and we're constantly amazed at how long a page will stay on Page One, or even at position one, without a single revision or update. With PBM, your content really does become an appreciating asset, growing increasing revenue over time with decreasing investment.

That said, constant surveillance and improvement of your content can only make your position stronger. Keeping your eye on ranking and engagement data ensures that you are immediately aware if a particular piece of content is slipping or if your competitors are gaining ground on the topics you care about. The internet doesn't stay the same for long, and focusing on the metrics that signal true organic performance allows you to be responsive and nimble, making just the right corrections quickly and confidently at the right times.

Best of all, you know that every investment in improving a single piece of content will improve the whole network. Because of the network effect you've built among all the content in your Pillar Topic, any improvement anywhere within that network improves the performance of every other piece. That's value for money. It's also the solution to the anxiety marketers have felt for so many years. As one of our customers put it, "Everything we're doing here is contributing to our network, so there's less emphasis or anxiety about any individual piece." You can rest assured that your data will tell you exactly where to put your efforts, and when.

So here we are at the end—and the beginning. Because once you've seen the power of your first pillar, you'll want to start all over again and choose a new pillar, build a new strategy, and create content to get to Page One on all the other Pillar Topics you want to own. For the first time, you can go into the process knowing for sure that you'll be able to choose the one most valuable topic to own, create the right strategy and content to own it, publish it for maximum leverage, and see it working in real time through your metrics.

That is the opposite of guesswork. The opposite of anxiety.

That is quantifiable confidence.

A lot of our customers have told us how much better they feel with a truly data-driven methodology in place, how well their content is performing, and how great they feel going into meetings with the CEO, carrying data and success with them. It's great to hear, every time.

But our favorite feedback was the simplest:

"It works."

CONCLUSION

The world of digital marketing moves, changes, and evolves so fast that sometimes it can be hard to keep up.

Think about social media. A surprisingly short time ago, college students in the US would rush to get their ".edu" email addresses because only students at certain approved colleges could join Facebook. Early adopters would sit in their dorm rooms, excitedly sharing clever one-liners about their "status" with the few hundred other users on the site, feeling the thrill of being on the leading edge of digital engagement.

Today, social media dominates our lives. As of the writing of this book, approximately four and a half billion people use social media. Nearly 70% of those users log in every day. In 2022, companies are expected to spend around $63 billion on marketing across these social media platforms. Many of the colleges that made up the original cohort of Facebook users now offer certifications or even degrees in social media marketing—including Ivy Leagues like Cornell and Columbia.

Or consider web design. Back when Toph started his broadband business, all he had to do was set up a page, almost any page, and that was considered enough. "Build it and they will come" was the belief among the relatively few businesses tech-savvy enough to run their own sites. Now, anyone with an internet connection can build a website—and a nice one, too. Entire platforms exist to help individuals design their own online storefronts, purchase unique domains, sell products and services, and collect payments. Even the smallest business has a site that works better and faster than those laboriously built sites of the early 2000s.

And just like with social media, entire professions have arisen out of the need for better and more functional websites. With an initial website design running as high as $100,000 or more and annual maintenance running into the tens of thousands of dollars for many companies, marketers can't be amateurs in these areas anymore. Any marketing leader looking to demonstrate professionalism has to be at least conversant in web design and branding.

Every time a new digital technology or channel has come on the scene, marketers have scrambled to incorporate it into their work, trying one approach and another, throwing everything at the wall to see what sticks, and generally thrashing around until someone discovers a better way. Once it's clear someone has discovered practices that work, everyone else rushes to follow, and those practices become standard expectations.

That's where we are with search right now—the convergence point where guesswork approaches and "let's see what happens" won't work anymore and a better way is needed. PBM is that better way.

Initially, search was simply an attempt to index the internet, to keep track of the growing number of sites and pages that were springing up at an ever-increasing pace. Google wasn't even named Google at first: it was called BackRub because its main purpose was to analyze backlinks. But like social media, search didn't stay small for long. Today, the internet is a massive collective brain, and search is the MRI that lets us watch it working. Search is no longer just about weblinks. It's become our best way of understanding what people want and giving it to them.

Pillar-Based Marketing is the evolutionary next step in SEO. In ten years, PBM will be the accepted methodology that marketers take for granted as they engage with search engines to align with customers across the web. Right now, you have an opportunity to be on the forefront, the leading edge of a better way of doing marketing that aligns what companies offer with what humans actually want, need, and ask for. That's not just better for business. It's better for everybody.

MORE THAN CONTENT

In this book, we've covered the foundational elements of PBM, from how we got here to how you can implement PBM practices in your organization. Now is the time to go out and put it to work.

As you set out on your journey to implement the PBM methodology in your agency or at your organization, expect to see benefits far beyond better blog posts. True organic alignment with customers drives outcomes in every area of marketing and communications.

> PBM doesn't just drive better content. The PBM approach informs every creative choice we make, from webinars to on-stage conference presentations, to social media, email messaging, and display ads.

Embracing PBM will mean you are more plugged in to your customers and what they care about than you have ever been, and that will drive better outcomes across all your channels.

You will see improvements in your ability to engage customers in your email messaging because you'll be talking about the topics and questions they care about, in the language they are using themselves. Your paid strategies will improve because rich content keeps customers on your website, no matter how they arrive.

For that matter, you will see a distinct decrease in spending on paid search strategies because your organic content will be more aligned to your customers, which search engines will reward with or without paid search spending.

You will be able to apply the same concepts to your display ads (or "programmatic" marketing) because you will only run your ads on the websites that are most relevant to your topic and your customers.

We are still working out and testing all the future applications of PBM, but the one thing that's clear is that the PBM methodology makes you more aligned with customer behaviors and needs, and better alignment with customers improves your strategy across every area of the business. When your CEO invites you to help build the three-year strategy for the company because you now know your company's customer better than anyone else in the world, you know you've got your seat at the table.

MAXIMIZING YOUR LEAD

Reading this book puts you at the cutting edge of content marketing. You have the opportunity to take advantage of a paradigm shift in the exact moment that it is happening.

So how do you maximize your lead?

LEARN THE TECHNOLOGY

Right now, today, marketing teams are spending weeks or months trying to figure out customer behavior. If you want to automate that down to minutes, you can go to the DemandJump platform and sign up. It's straightforward and easy to use; you can get started in a few minutes and have insights into customer behavior, the content network, and your competitors' rankings right away.

One thing we hope you've taken from this book is that we are passionate about giving marketers the tools they need to succeed with PBM. We want you to create incredible, engaging content that drives Page One rankings, qualified leads, and sales and gives you the confidence that what you're doing will work.

The DemandJump platform is, to our knowledge, the only technology that makes this possible.

Become Certified

In this book, we've tried to give you everything you need to get started with PBM, from the reasons to adopt it to the best practices for making it work in your organization. But if you want to understand and implement these strategies on a deep level—and signal to the world that you're an expert in this cutting-edge area of content marketing strategy—you can pursue a certification through DemandJump.

You can get certified in PBM strategy, in PBM-based content writing, and more. Wherever you fall in the marketing team, whether inside an organization or at a stand-alone agency, certification takes your knowledge and skill to the next level.

BRING PBM TO YOUR ORGANIZATION OR AGENCY

One day, sooner rather than later, PBM will be the set of best practices marketers take for granted. As with each of the evolutionary steps in digital marketing that have come before it, those who adopt early will have a massive advantage. And that's not true only for marketers, but for businesses.

If you own or work for a marketing agency, this is your moment to bring customers something totally new, to introduce them to a methodology that will make them thought leaders in the areas they care about. Imagine showing your clients how to beat Microsoft or Amazon on Page One. We've done it, and the excitement of showing customers results after only a few days or weeks, rather than months or years, is hard to beat.

If you are an internal marketer in an organization, this is your opportunity to show that marketing can drive exponential growth and contribute powerfully to the bottom line. It's your chance to prove to your CEO that your content strategy is not based on guesswork, that it's as data-driven, as predictable, and as quantifiable as all the other areas of the business.

> Content marketing can and should be a business driver, a major contributor to the overall success of every organization. PBM makes that possible.

Now that you have the mindset, the tools, and the knowledge, go make it happen.

Or as Toph likes to say, "Go crush it!"

ACKNOWLEDGMENTS

SHAWN SCHWEGMAN, CO-FOUNDER & CSO, DEMANDJUMP

Shawn is now a fractional CMO for global brands that are leveraging Pillar-Based Marketing to drive quantifiable results. Shawn has an insatiable appetite for leveraging data and making sense of it to step on your competitors' air hose. He has one of the world's most brilliant minds when it comes to "Think Differently." The PBM methodology simply wouldn't exist without Shawn, and we are forever grateful to him.

HEIKE NEUMANN, GLOBAL VP OF DEMAND GENERATION, QUADIENT

Heike has been a marketing leader at some of the world's largest companies, including Oracle. Thank you, Heike, for writing the Foreword for this book. Your performance-driven approach to marketing is inspirational, and you have challenged us every step of the way to align with enterprises. We're honored to share these pages with you.

BILL GODFREY, MANAGING DIRECTOR, 4G VENTURES

Bill was the first investor in DemandJump. Without his support, DemandJump would never have existed. Bill was also the co-founder and CEO of Aprimo, a highly successful marketing automation platform that sold to Teradata for $525 million. Bill's visionary thinking and his leadership and guidance have made all the difference for our organization.

PANORAMIC VENTURES AND ALL DEMANDJUMP INVESTORS

Panoramic Ventures, thank you for believing in DemandJump as one of your portfolio companies. Thank you to all of our investors for believing in the company and the pivots it took to discover Pillar-Based Marketing and the bravery it took to focus on this new marketing category.

ADAM HELWEH, CEO, SECRET SUSHI

Adam Helweh is the marketer we built this methodology for. More than that, he's seen the potential in PBM from the very beginning and has done so much to push us toward excellence. Adam, thank you for your partnership and your scientific mind. You keep us on our toes in the best possible way, and we wouldn't have it any other way.

DEMANDJUMP CUSTOMERS

To our B2B, B2C, PLG and Agency customers including startup, scaleup and Fortune 100 companies across nearly every vertical, thank you for listening when you received that first phone call when we said, "Hey, we think we discovered something revolutionary. Want to try it out?"

BRENNAN WALKER, VP OF SALES, DEMANDJUMP

Brennan is the person who asked the question, "Could we apply this to content?" He is relentless in adding value to people every day. He started at the company as an intern and rapidly grew through the ranks.

DREW DETZLER, VP OF MARKETING, DEMANDJUMP

Drew is a fearless marketing leader who always wanted to go to bed at night feeling confident that the actions he and his team took that day would actually work. He has been instrumental in deploying the actions and measuring the outcomes from Pillar-Based Marketing and helping us refine the entire process.

AMBER PECKHAM, LEAD CONTENT WRITER, DEMANDJUMP

For nearly a decade leading to the publication of this book, Amber Peckham has been Ryan's truest friend and fiercest ally in the business of writing words for organizations around the world. Amber, you're the sister I never had. We've been through more together than a few sentences can ever convey, and through it all, I'm grateful for your inquisitive mind, your sense of justice (and humor), and your talent beyond belief. Thanks for sticking with me through some of the hardest times described in the first half of this book, and for everything along the way.

KAYLIN CORDOVA, VP OF ORGANIZATIONAL EFFECTIVENESS, DEMANDJUMP

In the moment that Pillar-Based Marketing as we know it today first began to show up in Ryan's work at Metonymy Media, Kaylin Cordova arrived to bring us to the next level. Through the explosive growth of our agency as a direct result of the contents of this book, through our acquisition by DemandJump, and all the way to the present day, Kaylin has been a constant source of structure, stability, and intelligence. Thank you for being you—and being so good at it.

JALEN MOORE, GRAPHIC DESIGNER, DEMANDJUMP

It's not an easy task to take a few words about networked data and Pillar Strategies and turn them into clear graphics that bring those words to life. Jalen Moore is an incredibly talented designer, to whom we owe a debt of gratitude for sharing his talents to help bring the ideas in this book to life in a visual medium.

DEMANDJUMP TEAM

Thank you for the sleepless nights, blood, sweat, and tears. *Literally all of them.* It has been an incredible journey, and without each and every one of you over the years, none of this would have been possible to figure out. Math, algorithms, machine learning, how to describe it, how to sell it, how to support it, and how to execute it.

METONYMY MEDIA TEAM

Thank you to the brilliant team of writers at Metonymy Media. You believed in taking the leap as an agency, powered through our acquisition by a B2B SaaS company, and helped refine the process of taking the output from Pillar-Based Marketing and putting it into action by writing content that ranks on Page One every day—even ranking above Fortune 100 companies time and time again.

LINCOLN DAY, TOPH'S SON

You taught me that I could love more deeply than I ever knew was possible. You are my rock through this journey, and you probably don't even realize it. Hopefully someday when you have children of your own, it will all make sense. I want to set a great example for you and try to make the world a better place for you to thrive. You drive me every day to be a better dad and a better person.

TOPH'S FAMILY

To my parents, Kelly and Mary Anne, thank you for teaching me my work ethic and how to think three steps ahead during all of those years growing up on the farm. To my siblings, Rachel, Michael, Nathan, and in-laws of the sibling variety, thank you for your support and love throughout the incredible highs and lows of my entrepreneurial journey over the last three decades.

KRISTEN BROCK, RYAN'S WIFE

Kristen, you supported me at every turn. When I was 23 years old and thought starting a marketing agency was a good idea, you put food on the table and believed in me. It was you and you alone who kept me going through those anxiety-filled years before we found a new way, and I owe everything I have built to you. Every bit of it. I love you more than I can ever say.

RYAN'S FAMILY

To my parents, brother, and in-laws of the parent and sibling varieties, I thank each of you for being an endless source of support and encouragement over the years. Each of you, in so many ways, has helped me keep focused on building something of worth, and the end result of that is found in this book. Without your sacrifices and your wisdom along the way, this story would never have been told. Or at least it wouldn't have had a happy ending!

ABOUT THE AUTHORS

CHRISTOPHER DAY (TOPH)

Toph is the CEO of Elevate Ventures, the #1 most active Seed and Early Stage investor in the Great Lakes Region and #20 in the United States. He is an innovator, entrepreneur, business creator, community builder, job maker, and wealth creator. Over the last 30 years, he has co-founded eight businesses in seven different sectors, with multiple exits to Fortune 500 companies. He has been a part of over $600 million in transactions across multiple sectors, including artificial intelligence, SaaS, hardtech, broadband, entertainment, investment banking, and real estate.

RYAN BROCK

Ryan began his career as a marketer at the age of 23 when, with no marketing or business experience to speak of, he founded the boutique content marketing agency Metonymy Media. Through grit and an unwavering belief in the power of storytelling, Ryan cut his teeth in the world of organic content and SEO and built a thriving agency driven by the power of the creative writer. Today, Ryan lives in Indianapolis with his wife, Kristen, and son, Charlie, where he serves as the Chief Solution Officer for DemandJump and waxes poetic about Pillar-Based Marketing to anyone who will listen.

.

Printed in Great Britain
by Amazon

21011200R00157